GOOD COUNTRY PEOPLE

GOOD

COUNTRY

PEOPLE

An Irregular Journal of

The Cultures of Eastern

North Carolina

NORTH CAROLINA WESLEYAN
COLLEGE PRESS

ISBN 0-933598-41-6   ISSN 1047-7225   LC 91-68531

Tom Patterson's essay on the Belhaven Memorial Museum previously appeared in an abbreviated form in the July 1989 issue of *The Arts Journal* (Asheville, NC).

Photographs in the Knick and Patterson essays by Roger Manley.

Photographs in the Wilson essay courtesy of NC Department of Archives and History except for that of the Montmorenci stairhall which is courtesy Henry Francis du Pont Winterthur Museum and that of Old Town Plantation by J. Chris Wilson.

Photographs in the Quigless essay courtesy Milton D. Quigless, Sr.

Front cover: Emerson Stowe "Fat" Winstead (1900–1943). Courtesy of Matti Barber Sloan.

Back cover: Belle Mont, on the campus of North Carolina Wesleyan College. Photograph by J. Chris Wilson.

This project is supported by a grant from the North Carolina Arts Council.

CONTENTS

EDITOR'S INTRODUCTION

WILLIAM CARLOS WILLIAMS wrote that good writing springs "from the shapes of men's lives imparted by the places where they have experience." "One has to learn what the meaning of the local is," he continued, "for universal purposes. The local is the only thing that is universal." These words make a good place to begin our irregular journal devoted to the cultures of Eastern North Carolina because they assert a direct connection between our (and anyone's) immediate surroundings and ultimate significance.

So many of us seem to have concluded that "reality" occurs somewhere else (generally, just behind the television screen) and that nothing meaningful ever occurs in our own lives. We have forgotten the meaning of the local. Listen to Henry David Thoreau talk about contemporary America.

> Shams and delusions are esteemed for soundest truths, while reality is fabulous. If men would steadily observe realities only, and not allow themselves to be deluded, life, to compare it with such things as we know, would be like a fairy tale and the Arabian Nights Entertainments. If we respected only what is inevitable and has a right to be, music and poetry would resound along the streets.

In the essays which make up this first issue of *Good Country People*, there is evidence that they have so resounded. Stanley Knick begins with an essay describing the Native American communities of Eastern North Carolina. J. Chris Wilson looks at the development of architectural styles in the eastern part of the state. Alex Albright's essay on black traveling shows illuminates the culture of black people in the first part of the 20th century. In this essay, music actually resounds along the streets. And

Dr. Milton D. Quigless's account of two weeks in a minstrel show, which follows it, gives a more personal account of that experience. Finally, Tom Patterson looks at the Belhaven Museum, convincing evidence, to this editor, that ordinary life is "like a fairy tale and the Arabian Nights Entertainments."

"What would we really know the meaning of?" Emerson thought he knew the answer to that question when he asked it over 150 years ago to a few students at a small New England college: "The meal in the firkin; the milk in the pan; the ballad in the street; the news of the boat; the glance of the eye; the form and gait of the body;" in short, the anatomy and physiology of the ordinary—"the common," "the familiar," "the low." Emerson saw "every trifle bristling with the polarity that ranges it instantly on an eternal law," an ancestor of Dr. Williams' "universal." Emerson's faith was that if "the shop, the plow, and the ledger" can be "referred to the like cause by which light undulates and poets sing," then "the world lies no longer a dull miscellany and lumber room, but has form and order; there is no trifle, there is no puzzle, but one design unites and animates the farthest pinnacle and the lowest trench."

We may no longer be as sure as Emerson was of our ability to perceive one design, but our delight in the possibilities of diversity more than makes up for that. *Good Country People* is founded on the notion that there *is* no trifle, that good writing can articulate and celebrate the cultures of tobacco and barbecue, of farmlands and factories, of tech schools and evangelical churches, of the various races, social classes, and genders which make up the coastal plains region of North Carolina. We encourage inquiries, suggestions for future issues, and manuscripts. These should go not to me but to the director of the NCWC Press, Marybeth Sutton Wallace, 3400 N. Wesleyan Boulevard, Rocky Mount, NC 27804. Let the wild rumpus begin!

Arthur Mann Kaye
Rocky Mount, NC
July 9, 1994

GOOD COUNTRY PEOPLE

NATIVE SPIRIT:
A PERSONAL PERSPECTIVE
OF NATIVE AMERICAN CULTURES
IN EASTERN NORTH CAROLINA

STANLEY KNICK

THE story of the culture of Native Americans, or American Indians, in Eastern North Carolina requires a look at several different kinds of information. It is not a simple story. Even to begin to understand we must consider at least six main aspects: Population, Groups, Activities, Prehistory, History/Ethnography, and Current Culture. There are many subtopics which could also be included; but these six aspects, if explored fully, would provide a good basis for the beginning student of Native American Cultures in Eastern North Carolina. Since both "Native American" and "Indian" are frequently used terms among the original inhabitants of Eastern North Carolina, I will use both terms here.

POPULATION

There are approximately 65,000 Native Americans in the entire State of North Carolina. Of that number, about 50,000 live in the eastern section

Miss Lucy Jane Oxendine, a Lumbee elder, teaches a young friend the art of beadwork.

of the state; that is, roughly east of a line which extends from Rockingham through Durham and northward to the Virginia line. This area is generally the Coastal Plain and the Piedmont Rim. These Native Americans are concentrated mostly in a few areas for long-standing cultural and historical reasons.

Robeson County has the largest Indian population, somewhere between 35,000 and 40,000 depending on which count one trusts. Census-takers have not always been well received, and there are numerous problems with counting people who are not full-time residents, which could slightly skew the figures. But for this essay it is sufficient to say that there are more than 35,000 and probably fewer than 40,000 Native Americans in the county. The immediately surrounding counties, Scotland, Hoke, and Cumberland in particular, have smaller but substantial Indian populations (greater than 2,000).

Other counties in the eastern region which have good-sized Indian populations include Halifax and Columbus (greater than 1,000). There are a few other counties which have small but fairly concentrated Indian populations (by that I mean more than 500 but fewer than 1,000). These are Warren, Sampson, Onslow, and Wake Counties. Thus, there are quite a few Native Americans in Eastern North Carolina.

GROUPS

In this context the word "groups" is used to mean not only tribes or nations, but also other kinds of Native American organizations. To begin again with the largest, we find the Lumbee tribe or nation, most of whom reside in Robeson and surrounding counties. Other smaller tribes or nations living in the eastern part of the state are: the Haliwa-Saponi of Halifax and Warren Counties; the Coharie who live in and around Clinton; the Meherrin of Hertford County; the Indian people of Person County; and the Tuscarora, most of whom live in Robeson County.

There are also concentrations of Indian people in some other eastern cities. For example, Fayetteville has a large Indian community and an urban Indian organization, the Cumberland County Association for Indian People. The Triangle area, in and around Raleigh, also has a size-

These Waccamaw-Siouan men "crop" tobacco, a traditional
Native-American product for many centuries.

able Native American community and the Triangle Native American Society.

There are numerous local and state organizations for Native Americans. The North Carolina Commission of Indian Affairs, which is a state agency under the Department of Administration, has as its responsibility oversight of the general welfare of the state's Indian citizens. There is also a North Carolina Native American Youth Organization, which consists mostly of Native American high school students from around the state. In addition, there are several groups made up of Native American college students on the various campuses. The leadership of the various tribes or nations, and of several of the urban organizations, also has a group called United Tribes of North Carolina. Beyond this, there are numerous civic, social, and religious groups of Native Americans who meet regularly in Eastern North Carolina. So again, it is not a simple picture— Native Americans are spread out all over the eastern part of the state, doing all kinds of different things.

ACTIVITIES

It is easy for Americans to use the stereotypes we get on television—the *Ke-mo-sa-be* kind of image. Although there has been much speculation about the origin of *Ke-mo-sa-be*, including among others the proposal that the word was really a Spanish phrase *"quien no sabe,"* I suspect that one day we will discover that *Ke-mo-sa-be* really means "honky" in some forgotten Indian language. But whatever it means, we need to forget the stereotype of the subservient, if faithful, Indian companion.

Native Americans are, and have been, involved in nearly every conceivable kind of activity: legislators, doctors, dentists, fire chiefs, basketmakers, potters, artists, policemen, business-owners, computer analysts, electricians, entrepreneurs, farmers, pharmacists, attorneys, teachers, preachers, nurses, administrators—every kind of activity. If you can think of it, there are probably some Native American people doing it in Eastern North Carolina.

The activities of the groups are also noteworthy. For example, the North Carolina Commission of Indian Affairs and United Tribes of

Arthur Richardson, a Haliwa-Saponi whipmaker, shows how to use his product.

North Carolina sponsor an annual Indian Unity Conference. This three-day event, usually held in the spring, is open to the public and consists of workshops on various topics and cultural events such as an arts-and-crafts contest and a powwow. The North Carolina Native American Youth Organization also has an annual Youth Unity Conference, held each summer.

Each of the tribes or nations has an annual cultural event or powwow. A powwow is really a gathering to have a good time, to celebrate cultural heritage—a mingling of spirits of people who share something in common. Some powwows feature dance and drum competitions, and there are usually traders on hand to sell traditional and modern Indian arts and crafts. These powwows are generally open to the public and lots of fun for the whole family.

The preceding sections are meant to provide a brief overview of some of what is going on amongst Native Americans today. But in order to understand very much about Native American culture, it is necessary to turn our attention to the past as well. Enter prehistory.

PREHISTORY

My wife always reminds me to make clear what exactly I mean by pre-history. It is a notion that carries with it some additional baggage which needs to be unpacked. The term may seem to imply that in pre-history, that is *before* history, there was *no* history. This is clearly not the case. What I mean by prehistory is, simply put, "before the white folks arrived." Native American cultures were held together in part in the thousands of years before Columbus, De Soto, and John White by their own attention to history—what we often call "tradition." But it was an *oral* history, not a written one. It is only with the arrival of the white folks that written history begins.

Native American prehistory in Eastern North Carolina lasted a long time. Indian people have been living on the Coastal Plain and Piedmont Rim for at least 14,000 years. Some people say that the time should be extended back as far as 20,000 years (Mathis and Gardner, 1986, among others), but for at least 14,000 years Native Americans have inhabited this

Two Cohorie ladies.

area. In 1988 we completed an archaeological reconnaissance in Robeson County, where we found sites that probably extend back that far (Knick, 1988), and there are other sites all over the Coastal Plain which date to that period.

The earliest group of Native Americans are called, by archaeologists, Paleo-Indians (which just means "the oldest Indians") (Willey, 1966). These people lived in small, nomadic groups, probably consisting of one or two extended families. They survived mostly by hunting, moving as necessary to find game. Their stone tool kit included relatively few types of tools; they are best known for their fluted or basally-thinned projectile points. The Paleo-Indian period ended by about 10,000 years ago (ca. 8,000 B.C.).

Following the Paleo-Indian period came the folks archaeologists call Archaic (Coe, 1964; Phelps, 1983). This is not to say that all Paleo-Indians disappeared and were replaced by Archaic people. In fact, they probably were the same people adapting to a changing environment, with new and different tools and ways of life, thus leaving a different kind of archaeological record. Beginning around 8,000 B.C., as the forests of this area gradually changed from boreal (dominated by pine and other coniferous trees) to temperate (including oak, hickory, and other nut-bearing trees), the Native Americans began to utilize the changing forest resources. The presence of nuts and berries made for an environment in which smaller game could survive, and in which the Native Americans prospered. The stone tool kit of these Archaic folks became much more complex, and included axes, scrapers, adzes, drills, blades, atlatls (spear-throwers), nutting stones and other tools, as well as the more familiar projectile points (spear and dart points). This was also a time of population growth, and during this period (8,000 to 2,000 B.C.) people became increasingly semi-sedentary. Instead of constantly following game herds, it became possible to remain in one place for longer periods of time, possibly for an entire season.

The Archaic period ended sometime around 2,000 B.C., and was followed by the Woodland period (Coe, 1964; Phelps, 1983). This phase of Native American "prehistory" lasted well into the period of European contact in Eastern North Carolina, probably until the late 18th century,

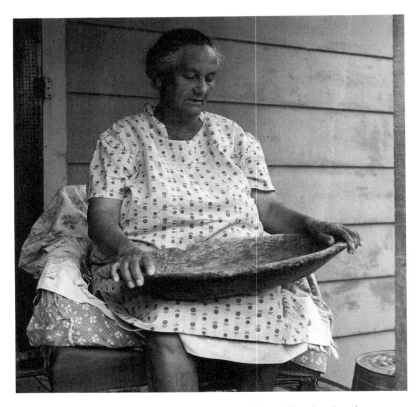

Miss Roberrta Locklear, a Tuscarora elder, with a handmade dough tray.

by which time most externally visible cultural elements had been replaced by European goods. The Woodland period is marked by major developments in technology and subsistence. The technological advances were the invention or introduction of pottery and the bow and arrow. The subsistence change was the development of farming. These changes had an enormous effect on what Native Americans were able to do with their resources. Now it was possible to settle into permanent villages, grow and store agricultural products, and develop networks of alliances amongst the various villages. While hunting and gathering were still important, farming became a major part of the subsistence base for many Woodland period people. Rich cultural diversity arose as the population continued to grow. Villages of 200 or more folks sprang up on nearly every stream and river.

Elsewhere in the Americas other cultural developments came into being. In the Southeast there arose a cultural phase which archaeologists call Mississippian (Willey, 1966). But since this essay is meant to concentrate on a restricted geographical region, and since there are few documented archaeological sites in this area which produce Mississippian components, I will stop with Paleo-Indian, Archaic, and Woodland as "prehistory" for most of Eastern North Carolina.

Of course, prehistory didn't end all at the same time in every area. European contact occurred over a period of many decades. A hundred years after Columbus, there were still many Native Americans who had never seen a white man. And at the time when there were well-developed cities on the east coast, such as Philadelphia and Charleston, there were probably Indian people in the west who had never even heard of white folks. Thus, contact and the beginning of "history" in North America took a long time to happen. When Verrazzano stopped in what is now North Carolina in 1524, there were possibly as many as 250,000 Native Americans living in Eastern North Carolina!

HISTORY AND ETHNOGRAPHY

History and ethnography have a lot to do with each other. Both are generally the writings of people who came into Eastern North Carolina from

W. R. Richardson, chief of the Haliwa-Saponi, outside his place of business in Hollister.

the outside. Both can be about the same activity. Technically speaking, ethnography had not formally been invented yet, but in my view many early travelers were practicing ethnography, or the study of living cultures, long before it was being called ethnography.

When the first historians and ethnographers came to the area, there were three principal language families present in Eastern North Carolina. (By language families I mean groups of related languages.) In this region there were speakers of Algonkian, Iroquoian, and Siouan languages. The Algonkian-speakers included the folks contacted by John White in the 1580s (i.e., Hatteras); most of these people lived along the coast. The Iroquoian-speakers included the Tuscarora, who occupied much of the inner Coastal Plain. The Siouan-speakers included the Waccamaw, and most of these linguistic relatives of the Dakota lived in the southern inner Coastal Plain and on the Piedmont Rim. Within each language family, there were numerous separate languages, and there is no good record of exactly how many of those languages there were in prehistoric times. This diversity of languages, in concert with the pressures of population decimation due to the introduction of European diseases and warfare, may help to explain why the native languages of Eastern North Carolina disappeared so quickly.

First, imagine that as a Native American you found yourself in a situation where being an Indian was a very unpopular thing to be amongst your new neighbors. And these new neighbors were fighting the Indians at every turn for control of the land. Secondly, your people were forced by disease and warfare into smaller and smaller groups; forced to coalesce into groups made up of folks from several tribes or nations just in order to survive and maintain Indian identity. English became, as they say in West Africa, the *lingua franca*; the language that everyone learned to speak. It was a language in which Siouan, Algonkian, and Iroquoian people could interact, without having to learn each other's language. It is quite possible that for an Iroquoian man, who had traditionally been at odds with Algonkian-speakers, learning to speak English was less of an insult than having to learn to speak Algonkian. In addition, English increasingly became the language of trade, which was very important to most Native American societies. Further, Native Americans were actively

Many Lumbee children find a cool place to have fun in the Lumbee River on those hot Robeson County summer days.

encouraged by their new neighbors to stop speaking their traditional languages. So, English became the practical language very quickly, and the native languages of Eastern North Carolina disappeared.

Each Native American community has its own particular history. In order to get very far in the study of specific communities, one needs to spend considerable time studying the history, ethnography, development, struggles, politics, economics, society and culture of a group. There are some comparisons which could be made between the communities, but each one has its own story. It would be simple enough to gloss over them all in discussion of their similarities; yet they are anything but all alike.

For example, the one I know most about (because we live in Pembroke and that is where I have conducted studies into the archaeology and history of the community and into the health of Indian children) is the Robeson County community. The history of that community is extremely complex. The best and standard work on the topic is *The Only Land I Know* by Adolph Dial and David Eliades (1975), in which much of the history is recounted. Perhaps one of the most fascinating episodes in the history of the Robeson County Indian community is the story of Henry Berry Lowrie.

Toward the end of the Civil War, the Confederacy found itself in need of manpower, and turned to conscripting Indian (in addition to black) men to build fortifications at Fort Fisher, near Wilmington. Among those forcefully conscripted was a young Indian man named Henry Berry Lowrie. Henry and a group of men escaped from Fort Fisher and returned to Robeson County. His escape, and a series of events including the murder of his father and brother at the hands of the Confederate Home Guard, led Henry to wage a guerrilla war against oppression which lasted until 1872. During this period, Henry and his band of mostly Indians, but which also included at least two black men and one white man, carried on a kind of Robin Hood war against the Home Guard and ultimately against the county establishment. Much of this story is told every summer near Pembroke in the outdoor drama "Strike at the Wind!" Partially as a result of the Lowrie War, as it is sometimes called, Indians of Robeson County were given the right to vote. Within fifteen years of Henry's mysterious disappearance in 1872, the Indian community had

Miss Lillie Green, a Haliwa-Saponi elder, shows off one of the quilts she has made.

successfully petitioned the State of North Carolina to build a school for Indian children. That school became the present day Pembroke State University.

That is just a brief example of how one could delve into the history of a particular Indian community. The same could be done in the Haliwa-Saponi community, the Waccamaw-Siouan community, or any of the other local Indian communities. There is a world of history, ethnography, and native spirit to be discovered in each.

CURRENT CULTURE

A part of the acculturation process for Native Americans all over the New World was the gradual, and in some cases rapid, disappearance of many of the outward elements of culture. Many of these things are what Americans think of as being Indian culture: clothing, dance, language, architecture, and so on. In Eastern North Carolina during the period from 1600 until late in the 1800s, a great many of these cultural elements disappeared because it was easier and safer to get along with the dominant culture without them. Especially following the Tuscarora War (1711–1713), and the other Indian wars which occurred in the colonies until the time of the American Revolution, being an Indian in Eastern North Carolina was extremely dangerous. Indians were killed or driven off their lands just for being non-white, and for being in the way of "progress." Thus, finding a place where other Indian people were gathered—an isolated place where there was a sense of community, of togetherness, of Indian-ness—was very important.

Culture is perhaps best understood as a system of shared meanings. When the traffic light turns green, we *know* what it means. Similarly, Native Americans in the early historic period *knew* what it meant to be Indian. The tendency of those people to coalesce themselves into communities, to hold onto their identity and not to surrender it, even though they had to speak English and dress in the European style, resulted in the presence of Indian communities today. Perhaps the most remarkable thing about Native American culture in Eastern North Carolina today is that it is still here at all. Given all that they have been subjected to by the

James Mills, a Haliwa-Saponi chair caner.

dominant culture, it is a miracle that there are 50,000 Native Americans in Eastern North Carolina now.

And they are still struggling. They are struggling for proper recognition as sovereign nations. Most of them are recognized by the state, although not all. The Tuscarora, for example, are still not recognized by the State of North Carolina. Many of the tribes or nations are state-recognized, but not federally-recognized. Or they are given—as the Lumbee have been—a kind of false recognition. In the 1950s the U.S. government recognized the Lumbee as Indians, but refused to extend to them many of the same rights and privileges given to other Indian nations. So it was a somewhat hollow victory; and it is against that same false recognition that they still struggle.

In the 1960s and early 1970s there occurred a re-awakening of Indian culture—not just in North Carolina, but all over the United States people began to remember that they had left something behind, and that they wanted to reach back and take hold of it before it entirely disappeared. What they were reaching back for were the outward elements of culture, the traditional manifestations of Native American society. Powwows and cultural festivals began to spring up. Kids began to learn to dance in the Indian way, and to make Indian clothing. Much of this was Pan-Indian in nature, meaning that it did not come from a single culture but from many Indian cultures. And this Pan-Indian re-awakening found its mark, too, in Eastern North Carolina.

Since then, Indian tribes have gotten themselves together into organizations, such as the Lumbee Regional Development Association and the Waccamaw-Siouan Development Association. These organizations address issues of economic development, cultural enrichment, and community betterment. They are going into the future with Indian culture, rather than leaving it as something in the past. Indian culture is not just something dormant in a museum—it is something alive and vibrant, with much to contribute to the future.

It is easy for some people to say that, despite the fact that 50,000 Native Americans live in Eastern North Carolina, Indian culture is gone. After all, where are the tipis and war bonnets? Surprise, surprise—Indian people in Eastern North Carolina *never* lived in tipis, and probably never

Marie Spaulding, Waccamaw-Siouan, "topping" tobacco.

wore the Plains-style feathered bonnet. The only people who had any use for a tipi were folks who lived on or near the western plains, who had access to a great many buffalo hides and who needed mobile homes. People who wanted to live in one place in a village in the woodlands had much less use for a skin house. Their houses were made of thatch, or of earth, or of other materials which were readily available in the forest. Some of them even used rectangular buildings made of logs, longhouses curiously like the later "pioneer" log cabins.

Similarly, other products which were originally elements in Native American life "became" European products. Tobacco is a good example. And many of the vegetables thought of as Southern foods are really Native American foods: corn, beans, squash, and peppers head a long list. Many medicinal products which were Native American "became" pioneer medicines.

But in spite of all the mistaken identity, and mistaken conceptions of culture, there remain some things which have always been Indian culture. They have not disappeared, nor have they diminished in any way. These are things which can be seen in many "traditional" cultures (as opposed to "modern" cultures such as Western Civilization). If one looks at traditional cultures in Asia, or in Africa, or elsewhere, these elements will be found.

One of these is the importance of the extended family. It is very common to find two or three generations of Native Americans living in close proximity, on the same land or "home place." Within this extended family, there is a network of sharing, a support base. Very, very few Native American people in Eastern North Carolina go entirely hungry. This is not to say that there is no problem with poverty, because there definitely is one. But in the Native American community there is almost always someone to turn to, Aunt Mary or Uncle Allen, someone who can offer something to eat, who can make the kinship network happen. Likewise, there are extremely few homeless people in the Native American community. Most Indian people have some kind of extended family network to depend on when necessary.

Another element of traditional culture which remains is the importance of spirituality. One of the things which travelers in the New World noticed very early in the historic period was the great importance of religion. Spirituality was not a Sunday-go-to-meeting kind of thing, but was rather an everyday thing. It was not necessarily in a church structure, but rather in the "big church"—the church of all outdoors. That kind of spirituality cannot easily be separated from the commonplace things of culture. And spirituality is still critically important in most Indian communities. I have never seen a more socially-involving thing than church in Robeson County. Nearly everyone goes to church. One of the first things I was asked as an outsider moving into the Indian community was "Where do you go to church—Do you want to go to church with us?" It is something that almost everybody does. But it is not only spiritual—it is social, it is cultural, it ties the economic and political systems together. I was raised in a devout Baptist church; both my grandfathers were Baptist preachers. But this is something different. This is something set apart.

Another element of traditional culture, which I alluded to above, is community identity. It is this feeling of identity that holds itself apart as Indian. Regardless of the kinds of duress that Indian people have been put under, they are still identifying themselves within, inside the circle, as Indian. And it is very important. It is pervasive. All the kids know about it. The elders talk about it. It goes back into the past, but it also comes up to here; and it goes from here forward. It is very much alive.

My favorite part of Native American culture is storytelling. One of the ways that the culture has always been spread and kept alive is through oral tradition. This is the original kind of history—the kind of history Homer (of *The Iliad* and *The Odyssey*) had. Homer never wrote anything; he told the tales. Indian people are still telling the tales of their culture. One of the most enjoyable and informative things to do is to sit at somebody's fire, or on the porch, or under the shade tree, and be told stories. Often there is little or no introduction to the story—you just realize that it is happening. And you may not even know the importance of the story until it is over. But storytelling is an important part of the culture. We had a storyteller come to the Museum where I work (The Native American Resource Center in Pembroke) last year, and there were several groups of school children in to hear her stories. The children were spellbound. You could have dropped a bomb next door and I don't think they would have noticed. The story has a power in the way it is told, but also in what it tells.

Let me give you an example. This is one from Peter Blue Cloud, the well-known Mohawk poet, and it serves several purposes. It shows how a story works. It is about how to view Native American culture; but it is also about how *not* to view Native American culture. It captures a piece of the essence of what this essay is about: native spirit.

THE OLD MAN'S LAZY,

I heard the Indian agent say,
has no pride, no get up
and go. Well, he came out
here and walked around my
place, that agent. Steps
all through the milkweed and
curing wormwood; tells me
my place is overgrown
and should be made use
of.

The old split cedar
fence stands at many
angles, and much of it
lies on the ground like
a curving sentence of
stick writing. An old
language, too, black with
age, with different
shades of green of moss
and lichen.
He always
says he understand us
Indians,

and why don't
I fix the fence at least;
so I took some fine
hawk feathers fixed
· to a miniature woven
shield
and hung this
from an upright post
near the house.
He
came by last week
and looked all around
again, eyed the feathers
for a long time.
He didn't
say anything, and he didn't
smile even, or look within
himself for the hawk.

Maybe sometime I'll
tell him that the fence
isn't mine to begin with,
but was put up by
the white guy who used
to live next door.
It was
years ago. He built a cabin,
then put up the fence. He
only looked at me once,
after his fence was up,
he nodded at me as if
to show that he knew I
was here, I guess.
It was
a pretty fence, enclosing
that guy, and I felt lucky

to be on the outside
of it.
Well, that guy
dug holes all over his
place, looking for gold,
and I guess
he never
found any. I watched
him grow old for over
twenty years, and bitter,
I could feel his anger
all over the place.
And
that's when I took to
leaving my place to do
a lot of visiting.
Then
one time I came home
and knew he was gone
for good.

My children would
always ask me why I
didn't move to town
and be closer to them.
Now they
tell me I'm lucky to be
living way out here.
And
they bring their children
and come out and visit me,
and I can feel that they
want to live out here
too, but can't,
for some reason, do it.
Each day

a different story is
told me by the fence,
the rain and wind and snow,
the sun and moon shadows,
this wonderful earth,
this Creation.
I tell my grandchildren
many of these stories,
perhaps,
this too is one of them.

ACKNOWLEDGMENTS

I want to thank Professor Linda Oxendine, Chairperson of American Indian Studies at Pembroke State University, for her comments about the manuscript. Also, I want to thank Mr. Roger Manley for providing the excellent photographs for this essay; and Mr. Peter Blue Cloud, the great Mohawk poet, for the use of "The Old Man's Lazy." Thanks also to my wife, Susan Young, for her valuable logistical and anthropological assistance. And special thanks to the Native American people of North Carolina whose very lives and spirit are the inspiration for my work. Finally, thanks to the Great Spirit, for opening the doors.

REFERENCES CITED

Coe, Joffre
  1964   The Formative Cultures of the Carolina Piedmont. *Transactions of the American Philosophical Society*, new series Vol. 54 (5); Philadelphia.
Dial, Adolph and David Eliades
  1975   *The Only Land I Know*. Indian Historian Press; San Francisco.
Knick, Stanley
  1988   *Robeson Trails Archaeological Survey: Reconnaissance in Robeson County*. Native American Resource Center, Pembroke State University; Pembroke, N.C.
Mathis, Mark and Paul Gardner
  1986   Archaeological survey of the proposed North Carolina Indian Cultural Center, Robeson County, N.C. Ms. on file at Office of State Archaeology.
Phelps, David
  1983   Archaeology of the North Carolina coast and coastal plain: problems and hypotheses. In, *The Prehistory of North Carolina: An Archaeological Symposium* (M. Mathis and P. Gardner, eds.); N.C. Division of Archives and History; Raleigh.
Willey, Gordon
  1966   *An Introduction to North American Archaeology, Volume 1, North and Middle America*. Prentice Hall; Englewood Cliffs, N.J.

Figure 1. Montmorenci stairhall.

THE ARCHITECTURE OF EASTERN NORTH CAROLINA IN THE ANTEBELLUM PERIOD— A PRIMER ON FORM AND BEAUTY

J. CHRIS WILSON

THE fame of the architecture of Eastern North Carolina is most easily measured by the high regard that museums of national importance have held for its significant architectural interiors. Not only must one travel to Wilmington, Delaware, to experience the breathtaking sweep of the Montmorenci staircase from Warren County, but one must travel to the Brooklyn Museum in New York to see the extraordinary interiors removed from the Cupola House in Edenton. These museums have sought architectural interiors of distinction to enhance the display of their important collections of decorative arts. The loss of these interiors for Eastern North Carolina then is paradoxical, as it has contributed to the fame of the architectural resources of the state.

The free-standing or flying staircase from the Montmorenci stair-

Figure 2. Newbold-White house.

hall (Figure 1) is now exhibited in and often used as the frontispiece for Winterthur in Wilmington, Delaware, the most important museum for decorative arts in the United States. The stairhall from Montmorenci is the single most recognizable image associated with that museum. This freestanding staircase has become for many not only the most recognizable image associated with Winterthur but also the most beautiful free-standing staircase in American architecture. The stairhall came from Montmorenci in rural Warren County, North Carolina, and was built about 1820. The importance of the architecture produced in Eastern North Carolina is emphasized by the high esteem that this staircase holds.

EARLIEST STRUCTURES

Although the Cupola House is the best known of the earliest houses surviving in North Carolina, it is not the oldest. The house known today as the Newbold-White House (Figure 2) near Hertford is accepted as the earliest surviving structure in North Carolina. This historic site is usually advertised as having been built in c. 1685, which would endow the state with a single surviving 17th-century structure. There are those who believe that the 1685 date is more hopeful than probable when the structure is compared to others, especially in Southeastern Virginia, of the last quarter of the 17th century. A more likely and realistic date would be in the first decade of the 18th century.

The Newbold-White House is a small brick structure that incorporates most of the elements that we associate with "medieval" features. The geometric patterning of the exterior with glazed headers (the ends of bricks) and the restored diamond patterned leaded casement windows are its most distinctive features. In addition, the use of a water table, arches over the windows, the white bands just below the crown of the chimneys, and the gable ends projecting above the end walls all contribute to the "medieval" flavor. The interior has been extensively recreated but there is some original detailing remaining at the second level.

Traditionally believed to be the oldest surviving frame dwelling in North Carolina, the Cupola House (Figure 3) in Edenton has been for a very long time touted as the finest Jacobean frame structure south of

Figure 3. Cupola House.

Connecticut. Although not built during the Jacobean Period (named for English monarch James I, 1603–1625), the Cupola House exterior exhibits those characteristics that we associate with the style. The overhanging second story with supporting brackets, the central gable with lozenge shaped window, and the massive end chimneys are the major features. Although the Cupola House was once thought to have been built about 1725, with the original interior woodwork being replaced in the 1750s when the house was acquired by Francis Corbin (the King's agent in North Carolina), it now is clear that the house was built for Corbin after 1756. It is these mid-18th-century interiors that are now in the collection of the Brooklyn Museum.

The absence of those extremely important interiors does not prevent us from being able to appreciate the quality and significance of the Cupola House. The replicas that have been carefully reproduced from those in the Brooklyn Museum and installed in the Cupola House effectively present an image capable of conveying the intent of the craftsman responsible for the astonishing interpretation of these Georgian interiors, which I will discuss shortly.

The earliest surviving interiors in their original structure were once thought to be in the Sloop Point House, near Topsail Island, in Pender County. Although the exterior of the Sloop Point House has been radically overbuilt, the interior of the earliest, original part shows the use of a handsome chimneypiece with pilasters and a straightforward treatment of the wainscot. The stairhall of the Sloop Point House employs the use of horizontal sheathing, or paneling. In New England houses the use of a substructure that "frames" each room and is sometimes visible in the corners of the room makes it easy to apply vertical boards by nailing at the top and the bottom of each framing member, while in the South the more customary use of vertical studs at twenty-four inch intervals makes the application of horizontal boards more efficient. Also in the stairhall is the remarkable, yet naive, rail with spindles perpendicular to the closed stringer of the stairs. The most recent examination by Restoration Specialists from the Survey and Restoration Branch of the Division of Archives and History suggests a post-1780 date for these interiors rather than the 1730's date that has long been accepted. The exclusive use of a type of nail not available until after 1780 provided this astonishing reevaluation.

Figure 4. St. Thomas Church.

Figure 5. Old Town Plantation.

The oldest church that survives in North Carolina is St. Thomas at Bath (Figure 4) which was built in 1734–35. The church is a small, brick structure that has been restored. The front may have originally had some type of hood over the door. Although the structure reflects some of the changes that have occurred through the years, the Flemish bond brickwork with glazed headers, paved floor, and box pews help the visitor visualize an early religious space.

Probably the earliest inland house to survive is Old Town Plantation (Figure 5). Built in 1742 in Edgecombe County, it is on the Tar River just a few miles below the falls near Rocky Mount. The house has a gambrel roof where the steep side of the roof covers the second story, three pedimented dormers on the front and three on the rear, double front doors, and restored piazza rooms which open onto the porch rather than into the dwelling. These are the earliest documented piazza rooms in the state. They probably were used for storage or unheated sleeping rooms. Piazza rooms became quite common in later periods. The double front doors on Old Town Plantation reflect the multifunctional nature of rooms prior to the 3rd quarter of the 18th century, especially in newly settled areas. There probably would not have been a separate parlor or living room, and the most important room in the house, in this case with raised panel wainscot, would have had the bed of the master and mistress of the house and would have also been used for entertaining and domestic activities. A drop-leaf table could also have been pulled out into the middle of the room and opened for eating. The double front doors would have allowed free access to both the larger room and the smaller room on the right without disturbing the occupants. The larger room has much of its original panelled wainscot. The smaller room has most of its original woodwork including mantle and horizontal sheathing.

THE GEORGIAN PERIOD

After about 1760, the quantity of surviving structures accelerates rapidly, and these structures demonstrate clearly the flowering of the Georgian Period in the architecture of North Carolina. Technically the Georgian Period would have begun when George I succeeded Queen Anne to the

Figure 6. Chowan County Courthouse.

Figure 7. Governor's Palace.

throne in 1714. The characteristics that we associate with the Georgian Style will be more recognizable after mid-century, however. These are nowhere more successfully asserted than in the Chowan County Courthouse (Figure 6) in Edenton built in 1767.

The courthouse is a masterpiece of harmonious, interdependent relationships that subordinate each part to the whole. The symmetrical facade with central projecting section creates a vertical focus that visually balances with the horizontal width of the building. The alignment of all horizontals and verticals establishes an academic order that asserts visual rules and expresses complete stability, a characteristic of the Georgian Style. The use of Greek Classical, Roman, or Renaissance elements as inspiration for design references is also Georgian. The structural form on which these elements are mounted, however, is more original than derivative.

The Classical pilasters (non-supporting columns) and pediment (triangle) that frame the front door of the Chowan County Courthouse introduce into this grid of horizontals and verticals a diagonal that is repeated in the pediment of the projecting central section and the hipped roof. These well proportioned angles create a visual emphasis that focuses our attention momentarily on the cupola until we are quickly reminded that the height is only visually successful when compared to the width. That relationship is further reinforced by the careful balance and alignment between the solids of the masonry and the voids of the windows.

Both the survival of larger numbers of Georgian houses of the 1760s and the many revival styles that have depended on the Georgian vocabulary, including the Williamsburg Revival Style that is currently popular, also contribute to the familiarity of the Georgian Style. The Owens House at Halifax, circa 1760, is a variation on the gambrel roof that uses a side-hall plan. The side-hall plan gives an asymmetrical facade, but compensates with an interior arrangement that successfully creates a varied and utilitarian space. The Joel Lane house in Raleigh, also circa 1760, is a center hall structure that was altered in the 1790s and is appropriately interpreted and restored as scholarship indicates it would have been then.

The reconstructed Governor's Palace at New Bern (Figure 7), c. 1767, gives us a sound visualization of the potential grandeur of the mid-18th-century Georgian Style in North Carolina. Tryon's Palace, so-called be-

Figure 8. Cupola House interior.

cause it indicates the contempt many felt for the colonial seat of government and for William Tryon, was reconstructed on its original site from a combination of archaeological and documentary evidence. The original drawings by John Hawks were followed, including, in all but one case, his indication of bed placement. Archaeological excavations which rendered information about exact placement of walls and probable materials used in the structure combined with the conjectural use of English architectural precedents have led to an interpretation that is probably the best visualization of a Colonial Governor's residence in the United States.

Those characteristics that we find so skillfully developed in the Chowan County Courthouse are also well expressed in the Governor's Palace as demonstrated in the original drawings of John Hawks for the palace. And, in fact, John Hawks may be responsible for the cupola on the Chowan County Courthouse which was not completed until the mid-1770s and resembles a drawing by Hawks for a cupola for St. Paul's Church, Edenton, but never used on that structure. We also find in Tryon's Palace the development of a single central structure flanked by a matching pair of subordinate buildings and connected by a curved colonnade. These flanking buildings create a spacial perspective for the main structure. This successful device is seen in many other structures including Mount Vernon.

The interiors of the Cupola House (Figure 8) in Edenton of the late 1750s reflect the mid-18th-century Georgian style more ambitiously than almost any others in the state. The importance of these interiors led to their acquisition by the Brooklyn Museum in 1918. The downstairs interiors now installed in the Cupola House were copied from the originals and, because of their high quality, allow an accurate response to the house. The impressive chimneypieces, pedimented doors with pilasters, and other monumental architectural elements indicate the heavy dependance on architectural patternbooks.

The architect who had an enormous influence on American architecture in the last half of the 18th century and early 19th century was Andrea Palladio, an Italian Late Renaissance architect from the 16th century. Palladio's *Four Books on Architecture* had an enormous influence as patternbooks. A surviving structure that exhibits many of the features that we

Figure 9. Burgwin House.

Figure 10. John Wright Stanley House.

now associate with Palladio is the Burgwin House (Figure 9), c. 1771, in Wilmington. In fact, doorways (or windows) like the front door of the Burgwin House are generally referred to as "a Palladian door." They are usually characterized by a central section surmounted by a half circle and flanked by smaller vertical components separated by pilasters. The window in the ballroom that was added in the late 18th century at Mount Vernon is a famous Palladian window.

The John Wright Stanley House (Figure 10) in New Bern was begun in 1779 and visually offers a transition from the Georgian Style to the Federal Style. Although Georgian, the facade in mass and in detail reflects a movement away from the weightiness that we associate with the Georgian Style and a development toward the lightness that we more associate with the Federal Style.

THE FEDERAL STYLE

The Federal Style actually begins with the Revolution and continues until about 1820 or 1825. After the Revolution we no longer identify the architectural styles with the English monarchs who reigned during that period. The Federal Period is characterized by a tendency to emphasize the linear elements of a building rather than its mass which results in a visually lighter effect. Oftentimes the windows are a more dominant element of the facade than is the space between the windows. The sculptural mass is also diminished by less projection and recession than we find in the Georgian Style. It therefore appears flatter with more linear details to enliven the surface rather than having the sculptural projection that creates a monumental effect. In Federal buildings, elegance and refinement are more important than monumentality and stability.

The Eli Smallwood House in New Bern, c. 1810, reflects these characteristics. It is a side-hall plan that takes advantage of the use of a side garden on a city lot. The porch reflects the shapes that we would associate with Palladio and the details including the colonettes, dentils, and surrounds are much more delicate than we would expect in the Georgian Style. The interior, especially the second-story parlor (Figure 11), uses architectural elements including the broken-arch pediment with pilasters

Figure 11. Eli Smallwood House interior.

and the multiple registers of dentils and modillions on the chimneypiece and the flanking windows. (Dentils are those rows of continuous blocks that resemble jack-o'-lantern teeth; modillions are those larger blocks that are applied individually and are often more widely spaced and project from the wall and are perpendicular to it.) The cornice of the room also has multiple registers of dentils and modillions. The overall effect, however, is that the wall is visually neither pierced by these details nor do they project from it; rather they operate as a surface linear motif to divide the wall and thus reduce its visual weight. This produces an extremely elegant effect through surface manipulation rather than the architectural forms that compose the surface.

Although the Smallwood House is a side-hall plan, the more typical Federal Period house is symmetrical, either three or five bays (windows or divisions across the front), with a pedimented one or two story portico. The interior either has a hall-and-parlor plan (a large room and a smaller room with the centrally placed front door opening into the hall, the larger room) or it has a center hall with two roughly equal rooms opening off the center hall. The mantels are typically three-part mantels with pilasters down the sides of the opening. There is a freize (horizontal element) across the top of the pilasters that has vertical panels over the pilasters and a horizontal tablet in the center. In the more ambitious examples there are often carved sunbursts in the three panels. We also commonly find the introduction of rooms with specialized functions, like dining rooms. The Wilkinson House, c. 1816, in rural Edgecombe County attests to the very high quality of interpretation of the Federal motifs often used in rural structures. The availability of patternbooks allowed homebuilders or homeowners the possibility of successful results without the benefit of an architect.

Such is perhaps the case with Belle Mont (Figure 12) now on the campus of North Carolina Wesleyan College in Rocky Mount. Construction began on Belle Mont in 1817 as documented by the signed datebrick found in the east chimney. The structure reflects those stylistic features characteristic of the Federal Period in Eastern North Carolina including a symmetrical facade, pedimented porch or portico, articulated cornice, molded weatherboards, and the three-part mantels in the interior. The

Figure 12. Belle Mont.

Figure 13. Sally-Billy House.

architectural significance of the house lies in the survival of an important early portico and its highly developed cornice involving a course of modillions with multiple registers of dentils.

The aesthetic significance of the house lies in its sophisticated repetition of shapes that bring unity and distinction to the facade of Belle Mont. The repetition of rectangles in the window muttons, cornice modillions, and portico railings balanced with the diagonals of the portico pediment, the diamond motif of the portico friezes, and the crossed or "x" members of the railings bring a singularly coherent interpretation of Federal motifs to the region. The lunette with its keystone in the portico's pediment offers variety to the regimented concept. The rear two-story ell was joined to Belle Mont in the 1840–1860 period and was a portion of a separate structure.

An extremely interesting development of the Federal Period can be seen in the evolution of the tripartite form; if it is not completely indigenous to Eastern North Carolina, then certainly its advantages were readily recognized as a large number of tripartite houses were apparently constructed and many survive. The tripartite house probably derives inspiration from English Palladianism. A two-story center section with gable end facing forward is flanked by matching one-story wings attached longways to the center section. This arrangement allows three rooms with generous windows on three sides each for light and ventilation. There is also the possibility of a third one-story section at the rear which increases the function by capitalizing on the merits of a room with windows on three sides and at the same time increases the interior space by providing an additional, usually specialized room. The detailing of the tripartite form is typically Federal, with multiple dentils, modillions, and three-part mantels that emphasize the visual weightlessness and linear elegance. The Sally-Billy House (Figure 13), c. 1808, from near Scotland Neck and now in Halifax and the Joseph Tillery House near Tillery are examples of the tripartite form.

Somewhat related to the tripartite form in the Federal Period is the evolution of the Greek temple form. This form indicates additional interest in antique architectural styles that will later contribute to the development of the Greek Revival Style. The Georgian and Federal interest in antique

Figure 14. Elgin.

architectural styles was mostly limited to details while the Greek temple form indicates a growing interest in the precise use of antique architectural forms. The Greek temple form of the Federal Period is distinguished from the typical Federal form in that the gable end becomes the front of the structure rather than the long side as was customary. The use of the gable allows conformity to the major elements as developed by the Greeks in the Classical Period. The gable is transformed into a temple pediment; usually there is an entablature (articulated horizontal member), and pilasters on the corners of the structure are used to represent columns supporting the pediment. Frequently there is also a one-story pedimented porch that is directly related in form and detail to the overall structure and often resembles a miniature Greek temple. Elgin (Figure 14), c. 1827–32, in Warren County is a fully developed Greek temple form structure. In addition to all of the features presented, Elgin also has a pair of matching porches that remind us of the symmetry and projections that we observe in the tripartite form. The plan of Elgin transforms a side hall plan into a transverse entry hall that connects the three pedimented porches with the gable end entry. This creates an astonishingly dignified presentation. The sophistication of both concept and execution exemplify the quality demonstrated in the rural building tradition in the eastern part of the state.

Another of these astonishing rural buildings is Montmorenci, mentioned in the introduction. Montmorenci (Figure 1), c. 1820, was also in rural Warren County, the center of a highly developed building tradition in the early 19th century. Montmorenci uses several conventional late Federal motifs combined with modified Palladian devices, including the entry, window surrounds, and paired columns. The hyphen which connects the two parts of the house, however, is the location for the breathtaking, free-standing staircase and stairhall that is installed in Winterthur in Wilmington, Delaware. Although the installation is modified from the original appearance, the experience of seeing the installation and examining the documentary photographs taken before removal from the house allows us to exalt this staircase above the function of carrying people from one level to the other. In fact, it is clear that this was designed and executed primarily for the eyes and for visual effect. It is indeed rare when the product of men's hands elevates function or form to the

Figure 15. Bracebridge Hall.

level of emotional experience for the viewer. That has been accomplished here. Although this stairhall is apparently unique, there are buildings in Warrenton and the Warren County vicinity that relate directly in details to Montmorenci and surely are the product of the same builder. One of these is the Dr. Little H. Coleman House in Warrenton.

ROMANTIC STYLES

The second quarter of the nineteenth century saw a clear and decisive focus on romantic and antique styles as interpreted by builders. The first of this series of romantic styles was the Greek Revival style, an outgrowth of the interest in Greek culture that began in the political identification with them during the Federal Period. The development of the Greek temple form as one aspect of style during the Federal Period became the forerunner of the Greek Revival Style. The use of the pedimented Greek temple became the inspiration for most building. It was either used conservatively for the porch or more ambitiously as a basis for the entire building.

The characteristics that we find most frequently used in the Greek Revival Style in addition to the emphasis on the Greek pedimented temple are a shallow, hipped roof, a broad horizontal band or entablature below the eaves of the house, and the reference to Classical orders of columns, usually Doric (which is the most restrained). Door and window surrounds are molded and often have corner blocks with a circular motif sometimes called "bull's eye corner blocks." The typical rural Greek Revival structure that we see by the roadside in the eastern part of the state is a substantial, white, square structure with four rooms up and four rooms down, a room in each corner of the structure and a center hall at each level. There is also a shallow hipped roof, interior chimneys, usually two, a broad horizontal band beneath the eaves, and a broad overhang. On either side of the front entrance are side lights (window panes) and above the door are additional lights or a transom.

Many of the rural farmhouses, however, continued to follow the convential form used during the Federal Period but the details normally indicate their identity. Usually the pitch of the roof is not as high, even

Figure 16. The State Capitol building.

though it is a gabled roof. There is a symmetrical facade with either three or five windows across the top if it is two-story. If it is a smaller one-story house, it will have a door in the center with one window equally spaced on either side. The porch, if original, will always be directly based on the Greek Temple, usually Doric. The porch may have a pediment or may simply have a broad, horizontal frieze supported by the columns which may be fluted or not. Bracebridge Hall (Figure 15), the family homeplace of Governor Elias Carr, in Edgecombe County, was built in several styles with the Greek Revival front section being done about 1840. At first, this gabled end structure resembles many of the five-bay Federal houses that we find in the region. But the pitch of the roof is not as steep as we would expect in the Federal Period. The window and door surrounds are molded and have corner blocks. More than any other feature, however, we are captivated by the austere dignity of the pedimented Doric porch. The porch, which is a small-scale interpretation of the Greek temple, has a monumental visual impact.

The State Capitol building in Raleigh (Figure 16) was built between 1833 and 1840 and is among the finest surviving public buildings in the Greek Revival Style. The Capitol was designed by Town and Davis but reflects some modifications by those individuals overseeing the actual construction. The extreme monumental effect of the building is somewhat obscured by the great oaks that now surround the Capitol. Although the monumental effect and extreme severity of many features including its cantilevered balcony under the rotunda and the monumental orders of columns in both the Senate and House of Representatives are dominate, we should not overlook the amazing delicacy and refinement of the third-story stairwells. The interaction of the elliptical dome with the mock-arches is fluid and cohesive. The use of the Gothic Revival Style in several secondary areas of the building points up the acceptance of antique styles' ability to coexist and sometimes mingle.

The Gothic Revival Style is normally characterized by the use of the pointed arch or the lancet shaped window or door and other references to the Gothic Style of the 13th or 14th centuries. The style is used most often for churches since the major surviving examples of the Gothic Style are the Gothic cathedrals of Europe. Saint James (Figure 17), c. 1839–40, in

Figure 17. St. James.

Wilmington is one of the first Gothic Revival structures in the state. It follows many of the conventions that we associate with the Gothic Revival Style, having a tower with pinnacles, pointed arch windows and doors, and stucco over brick to resemble the stone cathedrals. Christ Church in Raleigh is another example as is Calvary Parish Church in Tarboro. Calvary Parish was designed by William Purcival and construction began in 1860 although it was not completed until after the Civil War. Calvary Parish is distinguished by the asymmetrical spires and brick surface which resulted from the delay in completion as stucco was the intent of Purcival.

Few substantial houses in the Gothic Revival Style were constructed. One regional exception is the Noble-Gorham-Fillmore House in Edgecombe County which was completed in 1870. This house uses almost every motif and form that we might associate with the interpretive use of Gothic elements. A more frequent use of the Gothic motifs can be seen in structures that we identify as Carpenter Gothic since they rely on wood rather than masonry or stone. In addition to lancet shaped windows, we will often find pedimented dormers, asymmetrical massing, board-and-batten surface, and elaborate sawn-work detailing.

Large landowners in the antebellum period seem more inclined to build in either the Greek Revival or Italianate Styles depending on local preference. Some sources differentiate between the Italian Villa and the Italianate Style. The Italian Villa will normally have a substantial tower and other references to early Italian Renaissance architecture. Both use other features including a projecting central section, shallow roof with broad overhanging eaves and brackets often in pairs, paired architectural elements like windows or columns, stained glass, a lantern, and the occasional use of the round arch especially in groups of two or three. When three arches are used in concert the central arch is usually taller and often wider. We also find the introduction of the new material of cast iron with a decorative surface treatment but having a functional or structural purpose. And townhouses will often have, as they also do in the Greek Revival Style, a third story row of windows that are not as deep as those on the first two stories, sometimes being square.

The Italianate style was most certainly the preferred style of the wealthy landowners in Edgecombe County in the last years before the Civil War.

Figure 18. The Barracks.

Among others, the Barracks in Tarboro and Coolmore just outside Tarboro testify to the ability of the style to attract patrons. The Barracks (Figure 18) was designed by William Purcival for William Smith Battle in 1858. The history of families often parallels the evolution of architectural styles. William Smith Battle was the grandson of Elisha Battle who had purchased Old Town Plantation in 1747 just five years after its construction and the son of James Smith Battle who had built a Greek Revival House near Old Town in the 1840s. He was the first of the Battles to move into town and certainly wanted to exhibit his ability to build in the latest style and wanted to impress people with the size and quality of his new home.

The Barracks, as it is called because of a Revolutionary encampment near the site, is a display of the latest style and visual effect in the years just before the Civil War. The occasional references to Classical motifs should not obscure the basic stylistic use of the Italianate vocabulary, even on such a grand scale. The interior rotunda was influenced by the rotunda in the newly constructed Capitol in Raleigh and the focus on visual effect which dominated much of the square footage of the house led to the need for a major addition in the 1870s to meet the needs of the family.

Coolmore (Figure 19), just outside Tarboro, is justly recognized as a remarkably intact and amazingly well documented grand house in the Italianate Style. The house was occupied by the grandchildren of the builder until 1994, and the house is testimony of the family's sensitivity to their place in the continuity. Much of the original interior decorative paint survives as does the path worn by small hands as they repeatedly trace the upward spiral from the first floor to the cupola. Some of the original furnishings are in place as they have been since 1860. The house is the work of Edmund G. Lind who was a principle designer of government buildings during the administration of Ulysses S. Grant. The environment of the house is enhanced by the presence of several original outbuildings that reflect the architecture of the house and the setting. The grounds, as does the churchyard at Calvary Parish, display that passion for botanic specimens, geometric forms, and romantic environments that was fashionable in the third quarter of the nineteenth century.

The coming of the Civil War had a profound effect on the architec-

Figure 19. Coolmore.

ture of Eastern North Carolina, as it postponed the completion of many building projects until the late 1860s or 1870s. Prior to the Civil War, skilled slave labor was used to construct buildings. In fact, the counties of Warren and Edgecombe that had the most highly developed plantation economies also had very highly developed building traditions in the years prior to the Civil War.

The most famous examples of the early architecture of Eastern North Carolina continue to be those that have enjoyed the highest profile, those that have become part of important collections or have historically received good publicity. They have, in fact, helped many to focus attention not just on what we have lost, but also on what we have remaining, both famous and obscure. They have performed the valuable function of calling attention to the extraordinary quality possible in the architecture of Eastern North Carolina. Fortunately, it is now much less acceptable to remove architectural interiors to install in museum collections or house construction than it once was. Our growing appreciation of the desirability of preserving in place is illustrated by the recent replicas used in the Museum of Early Southern Decorative Arts in Winston-Salem. Appropriately, the architectural replicas are used as the back-drop for the decorative arts collection and the originals remain in their Charleston structure. One wishes that the Cupola House interiors and the Montmorenci stairhall might have survived in their original locations. Ultimately, pride should also come from our recognition, appreciation, and preservation of that which we now have rather than that which we once had. Boasting of what one has lost seems to express only the pride in the architectural achievements and the culture which produced them and not also the pride in subsequent cultures, including our own, and their ability to recognize, appreciate, and appropriately preserve those architectural achievements.

Katie Bryant Abraham (r)
behind the *Silas Green* tent, about 1928.
(Courtesy of Katie Abraham)

NOON PARADE AND MIDNIGHT RAMBLE: BLACK TRAVELING TENT SHOWS IN NORTH CAROLINA

ALEX ALBRIGHT

IT'S been over sixty years since Katie Abraham and Dicie Pettiford danced onstage together. They sit in front of a standing room only crowd in a small Wilmington auditorium, trying to remember the names that go with the faces flashing on a screen before them.

"That's Johnson Rooks, married my sister—he was business manager," Dicie says. "Yeah, and that's Sam Gray. Oh, he was sweet." I'm repeating their answers to the crowd and showing the slides, which were taken from photos in Katie's album, nearly 200 candid shots she snapped with a Brownie, when she traveled with the *Silas Green from New Orleans* show from 1927–1932. The photos are mounted with tiny red hearts pasted on each corner, and they have enigmatic captions like "measured" and "sorry" written in white ink on the black pages. Katie lists the dancers shown in another slide, then giggles. "And that one on the end—you know who she is." It's Katie, tall, slim and beautiful, big dimples and sparkling eyes.

William "Geechee" Robinson (top center) with members of
Don Albert's *World's Greatest Swingband*, early 1930s.
(Detail of publicity photo, photo courtesy of Frank Driggs)

Katie had joined the *Silas Green* show with her first husband, baritone horn player Will Bryant, whom she'd met on the *Alabama Minstrels*. A slide shows him sitting at a portable desk, on a railroad track, and I tell the crowd his name. "Anything else?" I whisper to Katie. "That's enough," she says, "that's enough."

She and Dicie are flustered because they can't recall the names of the couple on the next slide. They're talking back and forth between themselves, trying to remember.

"They used to ride that trick bicycle, you know."

"Yeah. She'd be on his shoulder, wiggling all around—"

"But she got too heavy to get around his neck," and they're laughing now.

"Got so heavy they had to quit!"

"I was around them for years and years and I can't remember their names. Umm."

Both immediately recognize the next one. "Ooh, that's Princess. Princess White," Katie says emphatically. "Now she could *sing*."

"Turn the house out when she'd be singing 'Sittin on Top of the World.'"

The crowd loves it.

The crowds loved them back then, too, when *Silas Green from New Orleans* was king of the road shows, from the mid-1920s until it was absorbed into a succession of circuses and carnivals as a sideshow in the mid-1950s. During its glory years, most under the ownership of Charles Collier, it boasted many of the world's best performers, some on their way to stardom, but just as many content to work the Southern tent show circuit. With a show like Collier's, work was steady, six different towns a week, about 44 weeks a year. Every day they built a stage and erected their tent, then took it all down again. They traveled in a well-appointed Pullman, equipped with a full kitchen and cook—all practical necessities for blacks traveling the Jim Crow South where public lodging and restaurants were often closed to them. Even during the Depression, when few shows could sustain a year's tour, *Silas Green*'s tents stayed full—at 50

Charles Collier, about 1930.
*(Publicity photo courtesy
of Katie Abraham)*

Ladies of *Silas Green from New Orleans*. Princess White (r), about 1928.
(Photo by Katie Abraham)

cents admission while most others charged but a dime. Because they were paid regularly with cash, not promises, performers on the show boasted "the ghost walks every week." (According to Henry Sampson, "the ghost walks" derives from a time when managers were supposed to pay performers on Sundays. They traditionally made their rounds with cash in hand, dressed in white suit, shoes and hat. If the ghost wasn't walking, folks weren't getting paid. The phrase also suggests an ironic comment on the usual white-owned structure of the tent show business.) William "Geechie" Robinson, trombonist and band leader on the show in the late 1930s, echoes the opinion of most of Charles Collier's performers: "Charlie Collier was the black P.T. Barnum. He was a showman all the way. He didn't go into the business to *save* any money."

Collier hired the best musicians, comedians, specialty acts, singers, and dancers he could find. He traveled with 60–80 people, sometimes including extra dancers and comedians who might never work, but would be available as substitutes if needed. And he boasted always that his was a clean show for the whole family. He visited prospective dancers' homes and assured parents he'd take care of their daughters, that, in fact, if they misbehaved, he'd send them home on the first train. Mrs. Abraham remembers his discipline somewhat wistfully: "After every show, we went straight back to the car, every night except once a year. We always played Jacksonsville, Florida on Christmas Eve and that was the one night we got to go to the dance." Every Sunday, the ladies went to church, wherever they were. Robinson laughs as he recalls, "Sunday mornings, you couldn't tell the dancers from the boss's wife. I mean they were some stone foxes."

But sometimes even Collier made hiring decisions he later regretted. Peg Leg Bates, for example, wanted very badly to join *Silas Green*. "Charlie Collier said how he didn't want no one-legged man because it'd be a jinx," Mrs. Abraham says. "He wouldn't take him, but that's one man really made it, made it good. He was on the *Alabama Minstrels* with me. We ate breakfast at the same table every morning, and we used to put our legs under the table and pretend like his peg was running our stockings. He'd always buy us more. He told me one day, 'I'm getting damn tired of buying you stockings, Kate. I don't believe my peg done that.' We had a

Detail of *Silas Green from New Orleans* band publicity photo
in front of Pullman car, 1940.
(Courtesy of Katie Abraham)

Birdie Wheeler in lace
pannier skirt and headdress,
behind the *Silas Green* tent,
about 1928.
(Photo by Katie Abraham)

lot of fun off him. He was a good boy, and he could dance all he wanted to with that one peg."

Everywhere they went, *Silas Green* was special. In Bennettsville, S.C., a city ordinance outlawed "all tent shows except *Silas Green from New Orleans*." In Huntsville, Alabama, at a concert for Alabama A&M, the college bandmaster presented the show with his original composition, "Silas Green March." Their routes were fairly regular, so their arrival was eagerly anticipated, and the cast were often guests at dinner parties thrown by local residents in their honor.

"We hardly ever had any trouble," Robinson says, and Mrs. Abraham and Mrs. Pettiford agree. Mayors and sheriffs throughout the South rode at the front of their noon parade in their cars, usually with Collier—who sent them, promoters, and entertainment writers boxes of oranges from his Florida groves every Christmas. Collier employed three advancemen, practically unheard of, to provide advance notice of his show, one posting bills about three weeks before show date, another a week before, and the third the day before, but the noon parade was the official announcement that the show was in town. Sign-carriers and drummers chanted, "*Silas Green from New Orleans*, best looking women you've ever seen. While we're here in your town, we're going to turn it upside down." The band pranced in fancy uniforms, playing standard marches to perfection. "Lot of people put the show bands down," says Robinson, who also toured with Don Albert and Fletcher Henderson. "But *Silas Green*'s band, those cats could *play*, every one of them. You hear 'em, you'd never know they were a show band."

Showtime was usually 7 p.m. The band opened with an overture, several classical pieces, played note for note. The chorus dancers then appeared, usually six beautiful ladies, in elaborate costumes, often with the feature dancer's in a reverse pattern. "We had at least three new costumes a year," Mrs. Abraham recalls. "Every year they'd go to New York and get the latest ones available." The dancers' three routines in the show were interspersed with songs, sometimes ballads or popular tunes, but particularly in the 1920s, classic blues from Princess White and Evelyn White; with comedy routines; and with specialty acts like Coy Herndon, hoop magician, and the Woodens, trick bicyclists. The show usually closed with

Coy Herndon publicity photo, about 1922.
(Courtesy of Ozell Joyner)

a short comedy, a new one penned every year, featuring Silas Green, the dandy from New Orleans, Lilas Green, his straight man, and Savannah, the "wench," often a male comedian in drag. The plot was always negligible, usually just a frame for the comedians to showcase their talent. Ford Wiggins, from New Bern, played Silas for sixteen years. Robinson remembers him well: "He could walk out on stage and people'd die laughing, didn't have to open his mouth." After the comedy, the band would accompany the entire cast for a flourish of chorus routines and specialty dances in the "grand finale."

In most places, *Silas Green* played to audiences divided racially by a rope down the middle of the tent. Occasionally they played a second show, and sometimes they played theaters. Afterwards, in some towns there'd be a dance in the tent, and often on weekends, a midnight ramble, usually open only to blacks. The ramble was another tent show, but without the play and most of the specialty acts, unless they could be livened up a bit. It featured instead the singers and comedians, and the band in much jazzier numbers.

Most of the stars of *Silas Green from New Orleans* lived their performing lives in relative obscurity. A few alumni went on to more contemporary fame, mostly because they recorded: Bessie Smith, Ida Cox, Ma Rainey, Muddy Waters, Monette Moore, Nipsy Russell, and Gatemouth Brown. But others, like Coy Herndon, sustained the show, performing on it for years. Ozell "Dollar Bill" Joyner, who began his professional career as a comedian with the *Rabbit Foot Minstrels* in 1917 and later worked with *Silas Green*, became visibly excited when he showed me a photo of Herndon and tried to explain his act: "This is the world's greatest hoop roller. See, he could make those twenty hoops roll—he's the world's greatest. Takes three ropes, one, two, put't on the ground, one three, one four, tied on his fingers. Got one hoop hooked to the top. As he waves his hand that hoop will come down and get on each one of them, and roll and jump up on his arm. That hoop starts them all off, starts 'em running around the stage, then he sits right down and they all come and crawl right over him. Then he makes them get in rotations and they all on top o' one another."

It may not be possible to understand exactly what magic Herndon did

Winstead's Mighty Minstrels band publicity photo,
1937, with Frank Sloan far left.
(Courtesy of Mattie Barber Sloan)

with his hoops, but everyone who saw him remembers his performances with awe. Likewise Ford Wiggins, Princess White, Ada L. "Ma" Booker, actress and singer; Frank Kirk and Daybreak Nelson, comedians; and Boisey deLegges, who played his "bottle-o-phone," a xylophone made of bottles. Yet, they brought top rate live entertainment—the latest songs, dances, and jokes—to thousands of Americans. They were particularly important to black communities throughout the South as role models, as exemplary and important people who could move with relative ease in a Jim Crow world. Tapdancer Lon Chaney, now starring in Broadway's *Black and Blue*, remembers his first *Silas Green* parade vividly: "They were the first live band I ever saw, and there they were, just marching down the street!" For people like Chaney and Mattie Barber Sloan, the stars of shows like *Silas Green* also offered hope of avenues of escape from the menial domestic and agriculture jobs many blacks were relegated to.

Mattie Barber finished high school in Laurinburg in 1930 and wanted to go to college. But she couldn't afford the $15 a month needed to attend Shaw in Raleigh, so she moved there and went to work in a local (white) doctor's home. But soon she gave that up, to sell tickets at the Rex Theater there. "I worked matinees and when they had vaudeville at night, I worked then, too," she remembers. But that job didn't last long, either.

Emerson Stowe "Fat" Winstead had just gotten out of North Carolina's Central Prison in Raleigh in April of '31: a year-and-a-day for bootlegging. He'd had earlier connections in the entertainment business, besides his interests in cockfights and gambling, and had already arranged to join *Dr. Robertson's Medicine Show*, out of Wilmington, when he got out. Robertson and Frank Sloan, a musician wanting to put together a band, went to pick him up as he was released, and the first thing they did was buy a $50 bus with money Winstead had made playing poker in prison. With the used Chevy bus, they could transform Robertson's little medicine show into a full-fledged traveling tent show, something on the line of *Silas Green from New Orleans*, which seemed to be making for its owner a small fortune, judging from all accounts of his travels to Cuba, New York, and Chicago, vacationing and checking on new talent.

Mattie Sloan (l) outside *Winstead's* tent in Durham, about 1937.
(Courtesy of Mattie Barber Sloan)

Chief Iron Hand, trick bicyclist and fire eater with *Winstead's* and *Silas Green*, mid-1930s, with Jimmy on his back.
(Publicity photo courtesy of Mattie Barber Sloan)

With Frank Sloan as band leader, the show was assured of having first-rate musicians and entertainers. He had been playing tenor sax with some of the best black traveling bands in the country since the late 1910s, including Ma Rainey and the legendary (but unrecorded) P.G. Lowrey, and his connections would serve them well in recruiting performers left jobless by the Depression and the parallel growths of the movie and recording industries.

Fat and Robertson were both white men, one at the end of his career as a medicine show man, and the other just beginning his as one of the most successful promoters of black cast traveling entertainment. Since Winstead bought the bus, he got the name; besides, there was already a *Robinson's Silver Minstrels* on the circuit, as well as a *Robinson Brothers Circus*. Their first show was the Rex Theater in Raleigh. Mattie Barber sold tickets for their show and met them all that night, and when they left for Wilmington she was with them: Winstead, Robertson and his wife Margaret, two chorus girls (one who doubled as contortionist), Sloan and the band, and Mattie, as bookkeeper, ticket taker, cook, seamstress, talent scout, and eventually Frank Sloan's wife. When Winstead and Robertson split up a few weeks later, Sloan then became Winstead's right-hand man, and his reputation in the music world would eventually prove the basis for much of *Winstead's Mighty Minstrels'* 25 years of successfully touring the South, by bus, truck and car.

That first performance in Raleigh was barely a show, but it was a beginning. "We added some actors as we went on," Mrs. Sloan remembers. "We played week stands, and we always had an amateur show on Thursdays and we could pick from that. You'd get some good actors, some real good dancers. But most of 'em weren't professionals. They'd go a few towns and then get tired and go home." And there were always performers left on the road, victims of failed shows, failing talents, bad health or bad luck, to choose from. Winstead soon filled his show out to a full complement of about thirty performers and extras. His chorus line expanded to five dancers and his band to a dozen pieces. He added canvasmen and advancemen, to erect the stage and tent and post bills. And he added features like Jonathan English, hoop magician, and Chief Iron Hand, trick bicyclist and fire eater, as well as blues singers like Virginia Jones. "We

Mattie Barber Sloan
in Maxton, N.C., 1989.
(Photo by Alex Albright)

Trumpet player Martin Anderson kneels near where *Winstead's* tent
will soon be erected for performances at "slave" camp
outside Cuthbert, Georgia, mid-1930s.
(Photo by Mattie Barber Sloan)

had some of the best actors in the world," Mrs. Sloan says proudly, "but we also carried some of the worst in the world. Fat would pick up some of these people couldn't do nothing, and he'd carry them, find 'em a job putting up signs or selling tickets. Claude Dixon. He was supposed to be a comedian, but he was pitiful. He'd tell his jokes and nobody would laugh and then he'd go sit in the audience and wouldn't laugh. He might've been good once, but he'd gone down. We buried him in Raleigh."

Today, Mattie Barber Sloan lives near her homeplace in Laurinburg, N.C. with her dog Penny. "I always kept a cat or a dog for company on the road," she says. "I bought a German shepherd one time for a dollar, named him 'Pal.' He'd watch the show every night, had more sense than most people. But when the band played he'd crawl under the stage. Soon as the show was over he'd walk all over the place. I'd walk around with him, picking up razor blades and stuff—one time we found $300 rolled up in bills. And I had two turtles, Maggie and Jigs, I carried a long time. Jigs got away in Florida. I brought Maggie back home and one cold night she got froze. My sister was scared of her and wouldn't bring her in."

At 76, Mrs. Sloan is a lively and energetic lady who remembers much of her career with startling clarity, wit, and candor. Sometimes years blur, and sometimes the names are hard to recall, but she speaks with authority, recalling scenes in sometimes chilling detail. During World War II, she remembers picking blackberries in Georgia: "It was me and a couple of the dancers. We weren't paying attention to where we were going, just picking berries on the edge of the woods. All of a sudden I looked up and saw all these (black) soldiers hanging in the trees. God, it was awful . . ."

She remembers other scenes of terror—rednecks shooting up the tent, sudden storms and washed out roads and bridges, a hillside of graves flooding across a road outside Salisbury, Maryland. She tells of playing for a 1930's slave camp in Georgia, outside Cuthbert, although if masters of such camps were ever prosecuted, it was for "peonage": "We played there every year. They had a schoolhouse, a church, and two stores in-side the (barbed wire) fence, and they had the guards with shotguns all around. They let us set up outside the fence and guards surrounded the tent during the show. But there was a couple of kids that danced on our amateur night, Daisy and Johnny Johnson, and they were *good*. So Fat

Fat and Helen Winstead
(Tourist postcard courtesy of E. S. Winstead, Jr.)

gave this man $1000 to buy 'em out. He looks at Fat and looks at the money and says 'You want 'em all?' Fat says, 'Just get me them dancers and send 'em up to Columbus (Ga.).'" The kids danced with Winstead's for several months and then disappeared. "I found out later," Mrs. Sloan concludes, "they'd gone back to buy their mama out."

Winstead's Mighty Minstrels traveled a different road from *Silas Green from New Orleans*. Although they often played the same towns and used many of the same performers and acts in shows that were virtually interchangeable, they carried different reputations, and some different personnel. Winstead employed three white men, Wash Turner, Bill Payne, and Roscoe Grice, as bodyguards for the show. They, in turn, used the show as a traveling hideout from bank robberies, and as a place to pass their counterfeit money. The show sometimes traveled in stolen cars, transporting them from the Carolinas and Georgia to a West Virginia garage for distribution in the northeast. After the show there was always a game or two. And they usually carried moonshine with them, often sold in the form of medicine. Winstead's son, E. S. Winstead, Jr., remembers the formula: 5 gallons of white lightning, ¼ bottle vanilla extract, and six nutmegs. "They said it would cure anything," he notes, "and I guess you would forget about your ills if you took much of it."

Winstead, Jr., doesn't remember much about his dad except what others have told him: "He was from Marion, Tennessee, and he weighed about 325 pounds. He bought a brand new Buick Special every year. People said when he'd drive by with his arm resting on the window, it would look like a sack of flour. Mom had a special coffin made for him, and it cost $5,000 for the funeral. It had a glass shield over the top and it was vacuum sealed, so his body could be exhumed and you could wash him off with alcohol and he'd be preserved."

Mrs. Sloan remembers Winstead, Sr., well and with a great fondness. One of her sons was named after him, and her daughter was named after his wife. "Fat loved soul food," she says. "String beans, white potatoes, fried chicken. First time I cooked for him, he gave me $20, said he wanted me cooking all his meals. I had done two fryers and he ate it all. He just loved to eat. Beans, peas, fried okra—I think about him every time I fry okra. I loved cooking so much it was a good match."

In a world where few whites gave black performers anything unless it was trouble, Winstead, Turner, Payne, and Grice were outstanding champions of an odd kind of rural justice. Winstead didn't pay as much as others, like Collier, but he paid every week, and he always made sure performers who died on the road were shipped home for burial, or, if they were transient, he buried them in his own Fayetteville graveyard. The three body guards were often needed, though sometimes they intruded recklessly. Mrs. Sloan remembers stopping for food at a roadside tavern in southern Virginia: "It was a little half-moon town. A lot of them places wouldn't serve colored, but if it was a big order and they weren't busy, they might give it to us to eat on the bus. So I went in with Bill (Payne) and Roscoe (Grice). That man looks at me and says, 'We don't serve niggers in here.' Well, I said 'Thank you sir' and was turning around to leave when Roscoe pulls out his gun and cocks it next to that man's head and says, 'You just started.'" After the food was prepared, Grice and Payne told Mrs. Sloan to go on ahead, that they'd be along. When the show passed by a few weeks later, the place had been burned; locals said the owner had disappeared.

Turner and Payne were executed by the state of North Carolina on July 2, 1938, for the murder of a highway patrolman. For several months after the crime they eluded officials throughout the Carolinas. They were sometimes reported in several locations at once, as the S.B.I.s and F.B.I., who got them to 7th and 9th on their most wanted lists, launched massive manhunts. Several times they kidnapped people, who invariably talked about how nice and apologetic their captors had been. G-men finally captured them in downtown Sanford. The prison chaplain who visited them just prior to their execution said, "They are plain simple warmhearted North Carolina country boys who got off on the wrong foot."

"Payne used to talk about all his crimes," Mrs. Sloan remembers. "He said he stole fifty cents from his mama one time and she didn't punish him. He always said how he wished she'd punished him or at least told his daddy, and maybe he wouldn't have turned out so bad."

Sometimes it's hard to believe that Mattie Sloan could have survived traveling, off and on for 25 years with Winstead's, with no bitterness, but her eyes still dance when she talks about those years. She still radiates a disarming sort of innocence, and it's very clear she loved the people she worked with, and she loved her work. Although she claims to've never been interested in performing herself, it's easy to see a bit of the actress/singer in her as she relates anecdote after anecdote. She often recalls conversations in representative voices, usually deadpan except for her eyes, no matter how funny or tragic the circumstances. Her stories are punctuated by sudden gems of wisdom: "Men'll get 'em a good looking woman and then leave 'em first time one better looking comes along. But they're the easiest thing to fool if you ain't scared of 'em." She'll still belt out a blues if she's prodded, and she'll still brag a little about her dancing: "Mary (her sister) and I used to win contests in Raleigh and Durham. We both loved to dance, always had. I know I got a whipping from mama one time for doing the ball and jack on a Sunday. I liked those dances with the off-step, when you walk, then do your step. We did the airplane, the shag—we were doing that in high school before the Lindy hop, I believe. We had a opry house when I was a young girl here. I'd go watch the dancers, the snake hip, the Hoover. They had a hall on Dixon Street, too, and we'd go to prayer meeting and stop by there on the way home. I always thought I'd get caught, but I never did—just that once."

Frank Sloan had run away from home in Winston-Salem when a teenager to join *Ringling Brothers Circus* around 1912. "He used to say his parents couldn't stand the racket he made on that horn," Mattie remembers, "so he ran away. They found him after a year and made him come home, but he was making more racket than ever before so they let him go." Sloan played with the Ringling band under the direction of P.G. Lowrey, and later with *Allen's Big Minstrels*, *Robinson Brothers Circus*, *Sparks Circus*, and the *Dawnie Brothers Circus*, as well as with *Ma Rainey's Jazz Hounds*, before settling with *Winstead's* for the duration of his career. He and Mattie had three children, all of whom were raised on the show as musicians in the band.

Mrs. Sloan remembers many of their stars with a familial fondness, though sometimes all that's remembered is a nickname: "Red was on the show. He never wore shoes. They arrested him in Lumberton, put him in jail cause he wouldn't wear shoes. He was nice, but people just didn't trust him cause he wouldn't wear shoes. David Ray was a fine dancer.

Virginia Jones, blues singer for *Winstead's*, about 1937.
(Courtesy of Mattie Barber Sloan)

He died in Philadelphia, fell dead in the streets. He didn't know who his mama was but he found her, and then he died.

"And Julia Pepper, she sang the blues—'Oh child, that ain't right.' That woman could natural born sing. Virginia Jones, she sang 'em, too, 'I Cover the Waterfront.' Umh. She was better than Bessie (Smith) I always thought, but Bessie had gone down by the time we got her. Virginia come to the show with her husband, Willie Jones. They had a comedy act together, too, where they'd sing 'A Good Man is Hard to Find.' Willie gambled all her money away, and he got to where he wouldn't put the cork on, so Winstead had to fire him. He run off to Georgia with this young girl and she made him go to work on a trash truck. Three months later he was dead. Virginia stepped in front of a car trying to kill herself. Finally died back home in Wilson. But she could sing. It'd tear you up to hear her singing 'You Going to Need Me.'

"Sophie Glover was a chorus girl from New Orleans. She had a different man every night. Next morning she'd go put all her clothes in the trash and buy her a new set. Shakey O'Neill, we called him Pot Likker, he joined with his wife, Rose. He was short, had a great big stomach. If you saw him do the mess around, you'd die. He'd turn the show out, shaking his behind. I showed all the chorus girls how to do the shimmy, and Pot Likker could do it better than any of the girls. He picked up dances real quick.

"Shadow Hooks was from Macon, Georgia, a fine trombonist. Nice, too, but a stone drunk. Dropped dead in a parade down in Georgia. We lost five that year in Georgia. And we had a girl with us wouldn't eat, didn't want anything but three aspirins and a cup of coffee. She'd crumble them up in her cigarette and get stoned, I mean. Wouldn't know where she was."

Winstead's, like *Silas Green*, boasted its fair share of noted personalities. Pigmeat Markham worked for them, and heavyweight champ Joe Louis made $500 a week for a couple of weeks during a Fayetteville stay just to walk across stage once a show. "We had all these postcards they gave us to sell," Mrs. Sloan says. "We were a ten cent show, and we were selling post cards of Joe for a quarter. We must have had a thousand of them, and they never came back to collect the money." Bessie Smith, un-

Buster Price, *Winstead's* drummer from Richmond, Virginia, mid-1930s. *(Courtesy of Mattie Barber Sloan)*

Mose McQuitty, center, in detail of *Silas Green* band photo, late 1920s. *(Courtesy of Katie Abraham)*

disputed "Queen of the Blues," was working for Winstead's second show at the time of her death in 1937. "Frank went up to Philadelphia and got her out of pawn," Mrs. Sloan remembers. "He brought her and Rich (Morgan) back. She was making $600–700 a week. Carried a slop jar of money. But Fat and Bessie didn't get along. He couldn't stand paying her all that money. See, when you goes down, you can't get back and Bessie had been down. People didn't believe she'd be singing in a ten cent show. Then in Durham, this man come up to Fat after the show and says 'What ya'll doing there with that lady? She ain't Bessie Smith.' He was fussing, wanting his dime back. So Fat said he was letting her go." But Frank Sloan talked Winstead into changing his mind, sending her instead to Tennessee to join his second show; a few weeks later, she was killed in a still-controversial wreck.

But, like with *Silas Green*, many others were perhaps as talented as the ones who had moved on to northeast urban audiences. Some, like Buster Price, wouldn't go North. "We called him 'Fish' cause he'd eat fish for breakfast if somebody'd fix it for him," Mrs. Sloan says, "and he was the best drummer in this part of the country. He could've made some money, but he was like me, he just didn't like the North," where recording and bigger stage opportunities might've led to more lasting fame. Some, probably more so than with *Silas Green*, had drinking habits that kept them from better jobs; others simply disappeared into the night. Most of *Winstead's* biggest stars were veterans at the ends of their careers, but during their time, performers such as Archie and Marian Blue, J.C. Davis "the singing banjo player," Mose McQuitty, Walter Mason, Billy Steward, Diamond Tooth Bill Arnte, Snookum Nelson, Ford Wiggins, David Wiles, and Arthur and Fleeta Gibbs were top of the line, among the best money could buy. Today, their talents are hard to appreciate because few of them ever recorded, because of the ephemeral nature of their shows— with no print ads or reviews to announce or record their performances, and because so few people are still alive who remember them.

Some of those with *Winstead's* were too old by the time better opportunities for blacks in show business started opening up; others had always distrusted promises of fast money. They feared being stranded in a cold city far from home when a theater run suddenly closed, and preferred instead the regular earnings of year-round work on a show such as *Winstead's* or Charles Collier's *Silas Green from New Orleans*.

With Collier's show, performers got the added bonus of playing Florida during November, December, and January—good work in a warm climate. Winstead owned several blocks of houses in Fayetteville, where his show wintered, and there was always work there for performers hanging over until the new season. If not in local clubs, chorus dancers worked as prostitutes and musicians sold moonshine or ran games. Fort Bragg assured them all a steady business.

By the end of World War II, both Collier and Winstead were dead. Titles to their shows had gone to others, who for several years continued touring successfully. But by the early 1950s, with the added competition of television, the days of the independent traveling tent show were quickly ending, and almost just as quickly, it seems, people began to forget them. Although hundreds of them traveled the United States and Canada between 1890 and 1950, few have been documented, and even when they have, it's often been in error. Historians, for example, have noted Silas Green was an expert manager and that his show's home base on the Mississippi River enabled it to attract excellent blues singers. They've lamented the passing of its ownership from black to white owners when Collier bought it about 1921. But *Silas Green* was never more than a fictional character in the show's one-act comedy; the show, begun about 1905, was never based in New Orleans and rarely played there. Katie Abraham laughs when I ask her about Collier being white: "He looked white as you, but he wasn't. No sir, he wasn't." Winstead's has fared even worse, rarely warranting a mention in contemporary histories.

The black minstrel shows of twentieth century America were, nevertheless, major influences on how Americans were, and still are, entertained. They frequently brought blacks and whites together under one tent, and sometimes the rope dividing them came down. They offered blacks, particularly rural Southern ones, rare opportunities for travel, and for employment outside menial tasks. They were proving grounds for performers with ambition for New York stages, and a last refuge for those whose fame had played out. With their traveling bands, they took the burgeoning jazz and blues forms—before radios and records—to all corners of the country. They brought the excitement of big city vaudeville, with all the latest tunes and dances, to towns too small to support a theater, and they sometimes took with them that town's best and most promising talent.

Katie Abraham can hardly remember when she didn't dance: "Ever since I was a child I loved to dance. I kept it up till I could do it. Once I was on the street looking, you know, at the parade. I think it might have been the *Rabbits Foot (Minstrels)* or the *Cotton Blossoms (Minstrels)*. The manager asked me if I would like to go with the show, and I was really anxious to go. I went home and asked mama, and she said 'You put your foot on a show, I'll try to kill you right there.' She told me never as long as she lived would I go with a show. But every time she'd have company, she'd always ask me to dance for them. She was proud of me, but a lot of people thought show people didn't have a good reputation. That's what she thought. But I tell you, *Silas Green* was the cleanest show on the road.

"And it hadn't been three weeks after mama passed that I joined." Her first job was with *Roscoe Montella and his Radio Girls*, playing vaudeville on the Theater Owners Booking Association circuit in the early 1920s. From there, she jumped to a sideshow on *Reuben and Cherry's Carnival*, and soon afterwards to the *Alabama Minstrels*, where she met her first husband. They joined *Silas Green from New Orleans* in 1927, and Katie was soon established as the best dancer on the show. She did feature numbers, including comedy skits sometimes performed in men's clothes, and she coached the other dancers. "I could go and look at a show," she says, "and see those girls dancing and pick it right up. Some of the girls never could keep up. We called them 'sticks' and 'white elephants.' They were pretty, but they just couldn't get the steps and the struts. Nobody'd want to dance next to them." She retired in 1932 and soon afterwards married her husband of over fifty years, Tom Abraham.

Dicie Pettiford and Katie Abraham worked together on *Silas Green from New Orleans* for about two years. Dicie joined to get away from the small town she'd grown up in, and because she loved dancing and thought she'd love to travel. "Mostly I liked dancing the waltzes and two-

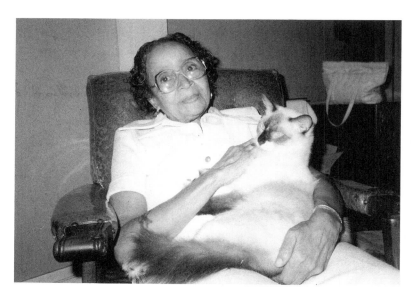

Katie Abraham (*above*) at home, 1989, with her cat Dino.
(Photo by Alex Albright)

Dicie Pettiford, studio portrait.
(Courtesy of Dicie Pettiford)

steps. The choruses were pretty but I didn't care for that kind of dancing myself. So I sold tickets, and I worked on the wardrobes, snatching and changing costumes off the girls while they worked." The travel, she adds, was nice, "but it was too much of it too fast. I never did like all the hustle and bustle." She married Leon Pettiford from the band shortly after she retired to pursue a career as a seamstress.

Dicie's sister, Birdie Wheeler, who later married the business manager Johnson Rooks, danced regularly in the chorus with Katie Abraham for three years. Dicie proudly points her out in a slide. At 87, Dicie has given up dancing. She's happy to be able to travel from her home in Hampton, Va., to Wilmington, where she's a little startled by all the attention she's been getting at the *Silas Green from New Orleans* reunion, staged there by the New Hanover County Museum. She and Katie have been joined by two musicians, James "Little Sport" Powell and Geechie Robinson, products of the Jenkins Orphanage in Charleston, S.C., who both played with the show in the late 1930s and early 1940s.

Someone in the audience asks what they thought about making history, and it's obvious none of them have previously considered such a question. Dicie laughs and looks to Katie. Katie, she's only 84, says, "Shoot, we were just dancing. And I can still turn 'em out when I want to."

Greenville, NC
May 1989

DEDICATION

"Noon Parade and Midnight Ramble: Black Traveling Tent Shows in Eastern North Carolina" is dedicated to the memory of Dicie Smith Pettiford, who was born in Carrolton, Texas on May 20, 1902, and died in Hampton, Virginia on June 24, 1989; and to Mattie Barber Sloan, who was born in Rock Hill, South Carolina on May 18, 1909, and died at Duke Hospital on July 3, 1990, after living in Laurinburg, North Carolina most of her life.

SILAS GREEN FROM NEW ORLEANS
1932 Route (partial)

April		June		Oct.	
30	Wadesboro, N.C.	1	Emporia, Va.	1	Scotland Neck
May		2	Enfield	2	Sunday
1	Sunday	3	Weldon	3	RockyMount
2	Monroe	4	Nashville	4	Wilson
3	Hamlet	5	Sunday	5	Nashville
4	Rockingham	6	Rocky Mount	6	Tarboro
5	Aberdeen	7	Tarboro	7	Williamston
6	Bennetsville	8	Wilson	8	Plymouth
7	Laurinburg	9	Dunn	9	Sunday
8	Sunday	10	Fayetteville	10	Eliz. City
9	Wilmington	11	Smithfield	11	Hertford
10	Chadburn	13	Raleigh	12	Edenton
11	Rose Hill	14	Louisburg	13	Washington
12	Wallace	15	Warrenton	14	Greenville
13	Warsaw	16	Henderson	15	Belhaven
14	Clinton	17	Oxford	16	Sunday
15	Sunday	18	Clarksville	17	New Bern
16	Goldsboro	19	Sunday	18	Beaufort
17	Kinston	20	Durham	19	Kinston
18	New Bern	21	Greensboro	20	Goldsboro
19	Beaufort	22	Winston Salem	21	Warsaw
20	Washington	23	Statesville	22	Clinton
21	Belhaven	24	Hickory	23	Sunday
22	Sunday	25	Salisbury	24	Wilmington
23	Greenville	26	Sunday		
24	Edenton	27	Charlotte		
25	Eliz. City	28	High Point		
26	Hertford	29	Reidsville		
27	Plymouth	30	Emporia, Va.		
28	Williamston				
29	Sunday				
30	Suffolk, Va.				
31	Franklin, Va.				

A NOTE ON SOURCES

This article would have been impossible without the gracious cooperation of Katie Abraham, Mattie Sloan, and Geechie Robinson. Over the course of many hours and repeated visits, they have shared with me the details of their respective lives and careers on the road. I'm also grateful to several other interview sources: Willie Jones, Dicie Pettiford, Birdie Wheeler, Ozell Joyner, Lon Chaney, Dr. Milton Quigless, E.S. Winstead, Jr., Evelyn Mitchell, Carl Foster, Raymond Pettiford, and James Powell.

Unfortunately, little has been published on the black traveling tent shows. Henry Sampson's pioneering work *The Ghost Walks* is a notable and invaluable exception. Most jazz and blues studies only sketchily document the traveling circuits, but four in particular add immeasurably to a better understanding of this complex and fascinating part of social history: Clyde Bernhardt's *I Remember*, W.C. Handy's *Father of the Blues*, Paul Oliver's *Songsters and Saints*, and Derrick Stewart-Baxter's *Ma Rainey and the Classic Blues Singers*.

Much of the additional information for this article comes from a survey of the "Entertainment Page" of the national editions of the *Chicago Defender* (1920–1950), J.A. Jackson's *Billboard* "Page" (1920–1924), and Raleigh *News and Observer* and Asheville *Citizen* accounts of the saga of Wash Turner and Bill Payne.

SOURCES AND SUGGESTIONS FOR FURTHER READING

Albertson, Chris. 1972. *Bessie*. New York: Stein and Day.

Albright, Alex. 1989. "Mose McQuitty's Unknown Career: A Personal History of Black Music in America." *Center for Black Music Research Bulletin*. Fall: 8–11.

Allen, Dick. 1970. "Don Albert and His Ten Pals." *Storyville* 31: 20–25.

Baker, Eleanor J. 1989. "Silas Green Show." *The Encyclopedia of Southern Culture*. Chapel Hill, NC: The UNC Press.

Bernhardt, Clyde E.B. and Sheldon Harris. 1986. *I Remember: Eighty Years of Black Entertainment, Big Bands, and the Blues*. Philadelphia: University of Pennsylvania Press.

Bricktop (Ada Smith Duconge). 1983. *Bricktop*. New York: Atheneum.

Bastin, Bruce. 1971. *Crying for the Carolines*. London: Studio Vista Ltd.

Daniel, Clifton. 1988. "The Show on the Road." Wilmington *Star*. February 12: 1, 3D.

Handy, W.C. (1941) 1970. *Father of the Blues*. New York: Collier.

Harris, Sheldon (1979) 1989. *Blues Who's Who*. New Rochelle, NY: Arlington House.

Johnson, John. 1954. "Silas Green of New Orleans." *Ebony*. September: 68–72.

McQuitty, Mose. 1937. *Routebook*. Held in the collection of the author.

Oliver, Paul. 1984. *Songsters and Saints*. New York: Cambridge University Press.

Oliver, Paul. 1969. *The Story of the Blues*. Philadelphia: Chilton Books.

Oxley, Dave. 1965. "Interview." Held at the William Ransom Hogan Jazz Archives, Tulane University, New Orleans.

Sampson, Henry. 1980. *Blacks in Blackface*. Metuchen, N.J.: Scarecrow Press.

Sampson, Henry. 1988. *The Ghost Walks*. Metuchen, N.J.: Scarecrow Press.

Sloan, Mattie Barber. 1955. *Route and Receipt Book*. Held in the collection of the author.

Stewart-Baxter, Derrick. 1970. *Ma Rainey and the Classic Blues Singers*. New York: Stein and Day.

Toll, Robert C. 1974. *Blacking Up: The Minstrel Show in 19th Century America*. New York: Oxford University Press.

TWO WEEKS ON
A MINSTREL SHOW

MILTON D. QUIGLESS, SR.

IN 1922, the Alcorn A & M College band was tops, and I considered myself to be a pretty good trombone player. I played first trombone and felt that I was equal to any trombone player in any college band. However, the time was not long in coming when I would find out that I was not quite so hot.

The first trumpet player in our band was named DeWitt Buckingham. We called him Buck for short. He was short in stature, but was a darned good trumpet player with quite a bit of experience. He had been playing his trumpet since he was about ten years old and would make a little extra change in the summer by playing with a minstrel band. It just so happened that the minstrel show had its headquarters in Port Gibson, my little hometown. The idea came to me to get with the minstrel band that summer so that I could make money to buy me some extra clothes for the coming school year, and have the experience of some travel, especially through the South and the southeastern part of the United States.

I asked Buck about my chances of being hired to play with the minstrel band during the coming summer.

John, Thelma, and Milton Quigless, 1907, Port Gibson, Mississippi.
Photo taken by a traveling photographer during the summer.
Milton Quigless is wearing a neighbor girl's shoes because
he'd worn his out and the family was waiting until Fall to
buy him a new pair when there would be
greater need of them.

He said, "You know the home base is at Port Gibson? Do you know Mr. Walcott?"

"Yes," I answered. "I know Mr. Walcott. He's the owner of the *Rabbit's Foot Minstrel Show*."

I was born in Port Gibson, Mississippi on August 16, 1904. Back in those days there were few outlets for entertainment that were open to blacks. It is true that there was one movie theater, where traveling variety shows also performed. As long as I could get ten cents together I would go to the movies. Of course, we had to go to the balcony, and couldn't enter the front door. We had to go down an alley to the side door. Later, they changed that and let us come in the front, but we still sat in the balcony.

Back in those days, William S. Hart was the main cowboy actor. We had serials, too. I remember the serial, *The Iron Cloth*, which was a horror serial. I think there was another called *The Perils of Pauline*. I'll never forget *Birth of a Nation*. It was very highly advertised when it came to town, and I went to that doggone thing. When they showed that lynching, the whites were cheering. I tell you we were suffering up in that balcony. Then when they showed Sherman marching down there and tearing everything up, they got quiet about that. But when they showed the whitecaps— that's what we called the Klan—and the lynching, all the white folks were cheering. They laughed at how they were treating us in that movie. And after it was gone, they praised it to no end. Everybody was talking about it. You could tell a difference in things for about six months after it was gone. They weren't exactly hostile, but you could sense a strange feeling. There was one white man that stuttered, and I'll never forget how he'd be down at the garage, saying "I love the way they treated the niggers in that movie."

Black people welcomed the arrival of the minstrel shows because it gave them something to laugh about. Life was rather tough on black folks back in those days. We certainly couldn't laugh at white folks. I had noticed that the older boys and girls were excited and elated every time notices were put on the billboards announcing the arrival of minstrels. I soon learned why such announcements were met with so much joy. On the day the minstrels arrived in town, there would be a great parade with a loud band, gorgeous banners announcing the arrival of the show, and actors decked out in outlandish costumes strutting down the streets, keeping time with the music, and smiling and waving at the onlookers. The actors would be wearing red pants with patches, or big striped pants, and a hat all torn in the middle. They'd wear frock-tail coats that were all raggedy, and these shoes that were three times the size they should've been. Of course they weren't real shoes, just part of the costume. They wore their regular shoes inside them. They had their faces blackened with black cork, and huge red lips. At the show, they would make jokes with each other, such as questions like, "Man, who was that lady I saw you with last night?" "That was no lady, that was my wife." Or you might hear the question, "Why did the chicken cross the road?" Someone would answer, "To get to the other side."

We had a neighbor who had a phonograph. We called it a graphaphone. This neighbor had some records of Bert Williams, a very famous black comic. However, he did not murder the king's English when he talked as did some of the other black comics at that time. I loved listening to his records and the way he talked. I can still remember some of his records. First there was one about ten little bottles. There was another, "Rev. Eatmore's Sermon on Generosity," and "Bring Back Those Wonderful Days." The one that intrigued me more than any other was "I Want to Know Where Totsy Went When He Said Goodbye." That was based on an opera, and I thought it interesting that he had taken off on the opera, because they appealed to whites maybe more than blacks.

When I was about twelve years of age, I heard the white people talking about the white minstrels which toured the South and performed in theaters. The white comedians would blacken their faces and put on the outlandish costumes. *Al G. Field's Minstrels* was one of them. They never performed in a town as small as Port Gibson. However, they would put on a show in Vicksburg, which was roughly thirty miles away. All the whites who could afford a ticket and the train fare to Vicksburg would go to see the show.

F. S. Walcott was a middle-aged man and stockily built. In addition to the *Rabbit's Foot Minstrels*, which Buck played with, he had bought *Huntington's Minstrels*. *Rabbit's Foot* was still going strong, but *Huntington's* was on the wane. Mr. Walcott was about 5'6" tall and weighed about 175 pounds. He had a very dignified appearance and was immaculately dressed at all times. During the spring, summer, and early fall, he was always on the road. During the late fall and throughout the winter he was home with his family. I think he had the only Cadillac in town. He smiled frequently and was easy to talk to. He met and talked with other successful and important men in the town around the soda fountain at J.G. Joseph's Drug Store, where they exchanged stories. He always had a good sense of humor, and a cigar either in his hand or his mouth. He wore big diamond rings on his fingers (at least I thought they were diamonds), and frequently would flick the ashes from his cigar in such a way as to exhibit his diamond rings.

He had a family. That is, a wife and after arriving in Port Gibson, they adopted a little girl. I have been told that his wife was once a circus performer as an acrobat. By the time she got to Port Gibson, however, she had gained some weight but still walked very gracefully. She was always pleasant and smiling and always had a word for the white people she passed by. The *Rabbit's Foot* showed there every summer, and after two or three years, Mr. Walcott had come back and settled. He'd come to town a few days before the show got there and have a big time with the bigshots in town. Then they bought a two-story antebellum house in the country. It had been the center of an old plantation. He also bought a service station, just across the street from the theater, where he and the bigshots would stand around and talk.

The Walcotts had two servants, a man and his wife. I was told that the servants had formerly been with the *Rabbit's Foot* a long time. Both were probably in their forties or fifties, and they always rode in the back seat of the Cadillac with the Walcott's little girl. Whenever the man was seen about town, he would be driving a little one-horse wagon picking up supplies for Mr. Walcott.

The *Rabbit's Foot Minstrels* started their season in Mississippi. They worked up into Tennessee, then down into Alabama and Georgia, and

up into South and North Carolina, and on into Virginia. They never returned to a town twice in the same year. During the winter, Mr. Walcott
began assembling his cast in preparation for his show for the next season. It was then that I came to know the performers. My mother ran
a boarding house, which was the next thing to a hotel that blacks had
in those days. My mother usually took in married show couples such as
Mr. and Mrs. Jolly Davis, and Mr. and Mrs. Brown. Jolly and his wife
were with the *Huntington's Minstrels*. He was very intelligent. I used to
love to hear him talk. But he could act the fool on stage. Mr. Brown became bandmaster on the *Rabbit's Foot*. His wife had the stage name of
"Sweet Georgia Brown." And she had a wonderful voice.

When the traveling black theatrical groups, such as the *Smart Set* group
based in New York City, began to include our little town to perform in
the theater, I was thrown into contact with such stars as Salem Tutt Whit-
ney. They had their own Pullman car, but he came to our place for the
food and to get away from all the mess. J. Homer Tutt always stayed on
the Pullman. I found the couples and stars which I met were all very intelligent people. I did not have contact with the single men and women
who made up the remainder of the troupe. The single men were for the
most part uninhibited, prone to fights, drunkenness, and various mis-
deameanors, and were responsible for the bad reputation the minstrel
performers were saddled with.

But the traveling minstrels and vaudevilles weren't the only music we
had. The colored people, as they were called then in Port Gibson, had
learned to appreciate good music and had a brass band composed of black
musicians. The leader was named George Comfort. My daddy played
baritone horn in the band, and all of the band members were a close-knit
group of men. One day, one of the band members left his trombone at
our home so I asked if I could play it. He told me to go ahead and try to
see what I could do with it. I began picking out tunes on it. Later, my
sister, Ruth, would come in and play the piano, and soon we made our
own duo. The next thing you know, I was picking out entire pieces that
were popular during that time.

In addition to the brass band, there was a group of men who played
stringed instruments, having what they called the string band. It was

composed of two violins, three guitars, two mandolins, and a bass viol. They played for dances, parties, and any other type of gathering. I was playing by ear and was going along pretty well. Subsequently, they included me in the group and I would make anywhere from $2-5 playing for a dance.

It just so happened that Mr. Comfort was chosen by the President of Alcorn College to take over the directing of the college band. In addition to that job, he was what we called supervisor of food services. There were about 500 students at Alcorn College and at mealtime anywhere from 15 to 20 minutes were wasted on getting the students in and out of the dining hall for their meals. Mr. Comfort—my father made me call him Uncle George because they were such good friends—found a way to get these students in and out in a hurry. He developed a small orchestra which would play a stirring march as the bell for a particular meal would start to ring. The students, both men and women, would march in, march to their assigned tables, and be waiting for the blessing to be sung in just about two minutes. Uncle George Comfort had charge of the dining hall orchestra as well as the college band, and it just so happened that the trombone player in the orchestra had graduated that spring. When I came around, Uncle George gave me the job of playing the trombone, much to the dismay of one of the band trombone players who had counted on that job before I got there. We received our board as payment for our services of playing at mealtime. Therefore, I was assured of my board from the very first day I got to Alcorn. And tuition was very cheap. I think it was about $25 a year, due to the fact that it was a state-supported school.

I really loved life at Alcorn. I was a new person and eager to learn. I enrolled in the shoemaking class, but Lord knows, I soon learned that I did not want to be a shoemaker. They put me to making harnesses. We had to sew the harnesses by hand and I did not know how to handle the tools. I pushed the awl with the palm of my hand instead of grasping it with my fingers and working it through the leather. After about three days, the palms of both my hands were swollen to such an extent that I could not hold the awl. Reverend Craig, the instructor, was a master shoemaker and would come by every now and then and give me instructions. However, most of the time he was making shoes from scratch for members of the

Milton Quigless in Chicago, 1927, in ROTC band uniform.

faculty or for some of the white people who were members of the Board of Trustees in Jackson. One day he stopped by my bench and saw me fooling around, doing nothing, and said, "Son, let me tell you one thing. You don't want to be a shoemaker, and you never will be a shoemaker. You are here just wasting your time and mine. Tell you what, you clean up the shop and I'll give you marks until the end of the year. Then I want you to change your trade, you hear?"

"Thank you Reverend Craig!" I answered. "You told the truth. I don't want to be a shoemaker."

There was another teacher by the name of Mr. Busby who came to us from Bordentown, New Jersey. Officially, he taught elementary agriculture. All the male students had to take agricultural courses. Mr. Busby talked more about current events than he did about cotton and fertilizers. He would look around the classroom and say that some of us are going to drop out when we finish high school. Most of them would be farmers. Most of those who went to college would be teachers, or they'd learn a trade. Then he said some of us were going to leave Mississippi. He said, "I can look around right now and pick out the ten percent of you who are going on from college to bigger fields." I thought that he was looking at me all of the time, and I was drinking it all in.

One day he told us that the school was going to do away with the civics class.

"Why?" I asked him.

He replied: "Because in that course we learned about the nature, or the setup, of the governmental process, from the city mayor through the county commissioners, the state legislature through the United States Congress. I tell you, I believe that the powers that be feel that in view of the fact that Negroes are not going to vote in this country, it is just a waste of time to teach them civics. Time could be better spent teaching them that part of chemistry that has to do with agriculture."

I will never forget those words. After that year, they stopped teaching civil government. All we needed was inorganic chemistry so we could read fertilizer tags and be intelligent about that. The teachers were furious, but what could they do? Nothing, but try to give us the inspiration to forge ahead and get into wider fields and do something for ourselves.

On one of my weekend trips to Port Gibson, I approached Mr. Walcott at his service station. As I said before, he was a very easy man to talk with. I told him who I was, that I was a student at Alcorn, and that I played trombone and was well-acquainted with Buckingham, a student who had spent three summers playing trumpet with the *Rabbit's Foot* band. I told him that I had been playing trombone about five years and that I was considered a very good first trombone player by my music teacher. I told him further that I would appreciate it if he would give me a chance to join his show during the summer, along with Buckingham. He said he would think about it and talk with Buckingham about me. The very next weekend I got Buckingham to come to Port Gibson. He convinced Mr. Walcott that I would probably add a bit to his band if I would be allowed to join the show.

Since the tour began in mid-March, it would not be possible for Buck and me to join the band before school closed in mid-May. Though Mr. Walcott already had two trombone players, he said that he would be glad to add a third and that he would pay me $15 a week. Now Buck, being a veteran in show business, received $25 a week, but that was perfectly all right with me. Fifteen dollars a week was much better than $6 a week working at D. Bock's Department Store.

Buck received two train tickets for us along about the first of May, and the day after our final examination, we caught the train to meet the minstrel show in Greensboro, North Carolina. Though I had been to Chicago, I considered a trip to Greensboro to be the greatest event that had happened in my life. The train ride took us from Port Gibson by the way of Vicksburg, Meridian, Birmingham, Atlanta, and Charlotte. We rode east through the cotton plantations of Mississippi and Alabama, through the foothills of Georgia, around and through the tree-covered foothills and mountains of South Carolina and North Carolina, and right on to Greensboro. Of course, we had to ride the Jim Crow car; that is, a half-section of a passenger car which was attached close to the engine just behind the white baggage car. During most of the trip, the Jim Crow section was crowded, but I was too busy looking out the window to notice and the time passed swiftly. We had no lunch with us; however, when the train stopped along the route, we were able to find a "colored" restaurant where we could eat any type of food from sandwiches to full meals of soul food—collard greens, hamhocks, black-eyed peas, and corn bread.

At that time, I did not own a trombone. However, Uncle George had allowed me to borrow the school's. It was a very good trombone, silver-plated with a gold plated bell, and it was in first class condition. I was greatly excited about the trip and looked forward to the time when I would be able to join a minstrel band and become a full-fledged trombone player. Now my real education was about to begin.

We arrived in Greensboro at about 11:30 p.m. The first thing we had to do was find a place to spend the night. There was no such thing as a hotel for colored people. They had to be content with so-called rooming houses. Most of the rooming houses had thin mattresses, and if they had springs, they would stick in your sides. In addition to that, bed bugs would chew on you from the time the lights were put out until broad daylight. Nevertheless, that was where we had to sleep. We were directed to a rooming house about two blocks from the railroad station. We knocked and a young lady came to the door. She asked, "What can we do for you?"

Buck spoke out, "We would like to rent a room for the night."

"Okay," she said. "Come on in. What are you doing in Greensboro?"

"We came here to join the minstrel show."

"Minstrel show!" the lady exclaimed with a loud voice and a look of disdain on her face. "Mama!" she called.

Her mother came out in her robe and nightgown. "What's the matter, daughter?" she asked.

"These two guys want a room but they are going to join the minstrel show tomorrow. We don't want them in here, do we Mama?"

Her mother said, "I don't guess they can find any place else to stay. We can give them the back room down there at the end of the hall."

"Mama, are we going to let them stay here?"

"That's all right. They need someplace to stay. We can't put them out. They're just going to be here tonight. They will be going out tomorrow."

After having come from Port Gibson where I had always been regarded as a harmless, nice little young boy, I now found myself in a situation where I was looked upon as something to be disdained and kicked out. I was beginning to get a little leery about how we would get along with this, but Buck was reassuring.

He said, "Ah, Quig, don't pay them any mind. After all, as you know, we are better than they are. Just don't let on that you know that."

We had arrived in Greensboro a day ahead of the minstrel show. However, we knew one person there, a young man by the name of Joseph Smith, who was an accomplished musician. He could play all the wind and string instruments. As a student, he had been allowed to direct the band and orchestra at Alcorn. He had taken the position of music director at Bennett College in Greensboro. We also knew one of the teachers at North Carolina A&T, Professor Garrett, who taught in the Agricultural Department there.

The next morning, we asked the landlady, who was much more civil than her daughter, to let us leave our bags and band instruments in the boarding house until we could find another place to stay. In the meantime, we went to Bennet College and got in contact with Joe.

Bennett College, at that time, was a co-educational institution that was founded and maintained by the American Missionary Association, providing facilities all over the South for the training of Negro youth. Bennett College was not very large and was about to be converted to an all-girl college.

The orchestra that Joe conducted was supposed to play for the graduation exercises that night. However, they had no trombone in the orchestra and the trumpet player was not so well trained. Joe was very glad to see us and asked us to join the college orchestra and play for the graduation. When the graduates and other students began to assemble, who do you think was on the fourth row? That same young lady who had been so nasty to us the night before. She ran over and was full of apologies. She said, "If I had only known that you were friends of Mr. Smith, I never would have acted so ugly last night." We accepted her apologies.

With Buck and me, Joe's orchestra consisted of four violins, two trumpets, a trombone, a French horn, a cello, a bass violin, a piano, and drums.

Inasmuch as Joe had been indoctrinated at Alcorn, he played the same type of music at Bennett he had been exposed to there. The graduates marched in to the strains of "Pomp and Circumstance." After a prayer, the next rendition was the Negro National Anthem, followed by the welcoming address by the president of the college. I cannot recall what music we played next, but then came the salutatorian address, followed by "Deep River." The valedictorian spoke next, and then the commencement speaker whose name I cannot remember. His speech was followed by the "Battle Hymn of the Republic," and then the diplomas were awarded, and the school song was sung. The commencement exercises concluded with the "Hallelujah Chorus."

Since we were already familiar with the music that Joe had arranged, I believe we added somewhat to the occasion, much to the satisfaction of the entire audience. And that same afternoon, there was a dance in the gymnasium at A&T College, so we went. The music was performed by what everyone called a jazz band drawn from the music department of the college. Since neither of us were so bad looking, we had no trouble finding dance partners. We did the one-step, two-step, and waltzes.

However, another thing occurred at the dance which led me to realize that minstrel life wasn't so hot. I was dancing with a cute young lady and she was really cutting the rug. She asked me where I was from and I told her that I was from Alcorn College. She thought that to be very interesting. We talked a little longer and she queried, "What are you doing in Greensboro?"

"We are joining the minstrel show tomorrow."

She said, "Oh, excuse me. I have a headache."

She sat down and spoke to the young lady sitting next to her. In ten shakes of a lamb's tail, I found that everybody had a headache. I pulled Buck aside and said, "Look here, Buck. What's the matter with me? All of a sudden nobody wants to dance with me."

"What did you tell them?" he asked.

"I told them where we were from and she wanted to know what we were doing here, so I told her we were joining the minstrel show."

"You damn fool!" he said. "Don't ever tell anybody that you're a member of the minstrel show. Don't you know that people don't like minstrel folk? They think that all of us are nasty, lousy cutthroats and thieves. We better go on home. We're not going to get any more dances this afternoon."

That was sort of bad, but he said, "Don't worry. You know who you are and you don't have to take their word for it."

Since the landlady's daughter knew that we were friends of Joe Smith, and word had gotten around that we were top flight musicians, we had no trouble remaining in the boarding house for another night.

The next morning the minstrel show arrived. They had a car that was attached to one of the local trains. The car was switched to a siding and we immediately went aboard. Mr. Walcott came out smiling and said, "Well, here you are, boy. Let's see what you can do. The parade is at noon, and we got to get ready to go." I smiled and thanked him. I was in high cotton right then and there. All the other members were seasoned musicians. They greeted me warmly, and Mark Veal, the bandleader, took me under his wing at once.

The lady who took care of the wardrobe measured my skinny frame and cut the costume down to fit me. It was a nice costume, light sky blue and modeled after a French army uniform, complete with a silk hat decorated with a gold-colored braid. The uniforms were decorated with gold braid covering the front of the jackets. There was a bright gold stripe down both sides of the trousers. I must confess that I thought I looked very good in that uniform. Of course, Buck's uniform was ready for him since he had been there the year before. But here is where my real let down came along.

We had breakfast and were just about ready to line up for the parade. The trombones were to be on the first row. They passed out the music and some of the marches I was familiar with. I said, "Oh, this is going to be duck soup to me. I've got it made."

Just about that time, Mark Veal came out. He was a famous band leader in that day and time. He was a dignified looking gentleman, with gray and black hair, and a deep rumbling voice. He had a stack of music and said, "Well, boys, I just got this music out of the post office and we are going to play these marches this time. All of them are new and you don't know any of them, but I know you guys can cut it."

I looked at the new music. I was puzzled and confused, scared, angry, every damn thing. I had never seen that stuff before. I turned around and said, "Mr. Veal, when are we going to practice?"

Everybody else looked at me. He laughed and said, "Son, what did you say?"

"I said, 'When are we going to practice?'"

"Son, we don't practice," he said. We do our stuff and you will catch it on the fly. Come on, don't worry about it."

Well, I was scared as hell because I was accustomed to practicing any new music until it was perfected. Even so, we lined up for the parade. I was shaking all over. We got down the street and I realized that I really was not a trombonist. I was just a scared amateur about to drown in a sea of professionals. The drum major waved his baton and brought it down and that started the parade. The drums started but they were not throbbing as loud as my heart was at the moment. We started the first piece and I think I hit about every third, fourth, or fifth note. Nobody seemed to pay any attention to it, however. After a while, I was going pretty good. I was catching on a little better and could play three out of every four notes. I was playing like hell, and all of a sudden it came to me that the music was getting faint. I looked around and I was marching in one direction and the band was marching in another. I had not seen the drum major twirl his baton to the right, indicating the route the parade would take around a corner. Lord, I was ready to go right back to Mississippi that day.

Buck said, "Look here, you can't go back now, you know. You have a ticket out here, but you don't have a ticket back to Mississippi."

Brother, I started studying that stuff. I studied all that afternoon and when the time came for the preshow concert under the tent, I had just a little bit more confidence. I made it through that show somehow. Anyway, after the show was over, I found that another great disappointment was in store for me. The railroad car that they were traveling in was half Pullman and half baggage car. The tent and all of the paraphernalia was stored in the baggage compartment and there were eight upper berths and eight lower berths in the other half of the car. That was all the space provided for 36 members of the minstrel troupe. The troupe slept two to a berth, which left four of us who had no berths on the car. Since I was the last person to be hired on the show, I was paired with a contortionist called Barrel.

Barrel and I went out and found our lodging for that first night in Greensboro. It was one of those typical lodging houses, lighted by kerosene lamps, with dirty sheets infested with bed bugs. That was the most miserable night I ever spent. The next morning we had to catch the train. The show car was so crowded that the four of us who could not find sleeping space in the car had to stand in the aisle. Everyone else in the car was sleeping late. We arrived and they fed us breakfast at about 9:00 a.m. and then I set out with my friend and roommate, Barrel, to find another lodging place for that night. We passed down a street and saw a sign that said "Room for Rent."

Barrel went up and knocked and a lady came to the door. Barrel asked her, "Do you have a room for rent?"

"Yes, we have one."

"How much is it?"

"A dollar a night."

"Can we have it?"

"Yes. Come on in and take a look at it," she answered. We did, and it looked sort of decent.

The lady then asked, "What are you doing in Salisbury, North Carolina?"

I said, "We are with the minstrel show."

"Minstrel show? Get out of my house!" she screamed. "I don't allow no minstrel niggers in my house. Bastards! Filthy, stinking, low-down, thieving niggers! Get out!" She even said that she was going to beat us up.

When we got out on the street, I asked, "What's going on? What's the matter, Barrel?"

Barrel said, "Don't pay them any mind. You know how it is. They don't think minstrel folk is any good at all. But we'll find some place to stay."

I was becoming more and more disenchanted with the idea of spending the summer being chased out of one chinch-ridden boarding house after another, standing up between towns, trying to learn all of that foreign music, and being scorned by everybody in the street who thought we were a bunch of no good minstrel niggers wherever we went.

But the *Rabbit's Foot Minstrels* was a good show, and we had a good band. Mark Veal played clarinet and you could hear him filling in whenever he felt help was needed to emphasize certain passages of music. I was at home when we played such pieces as "Stars and Stripes Forever." However, when we played more popular tunes with a march rhythm I had a little more trouble. Most of the music was marches and some of it we had never heard or played before. But the other guys were seasoned musicians and took to the new music like ducks to water.

When the band got to the center of town, we'd form a semi-circle and play something like the "William Tell Overture" or a Sousa march. Then Mr. Walcott would step into the middle of the circle. He had a regular spiel he gave. It went like this: "Ladies and gentlemen! I am the owner of the *Mighty Rabbit's Foot Minstrels*, the greatest aggregation of comedians, contortionists, vocalists, and top flight musicians ever brought together in one magnificent, stupendous, soul-inspiring group of veteran entertainers existing in these United States of America. You should consider your fair city fortunate to be favored by our annual visit. I would urge you one and all to be present at 7:30 p.m. when the curtain rises, and we present to you this stupendous group of individuals who will be glad to perform for you in our magnificent tent theater, which you will find located on the local show grounds. You have heard the magnificent rendition of John Phillip Sousa's 'March Under the Double Eagle.' As I came along I noticed that you could not keep your feet still, that you pranced and smiled and even laughed during the rendition of the most famous march ever composed, presented to you by our marching band. I would urge you to come, one and all. Meet us at 7:30 at our tent theater. I thank you, ladies and gentlemen, one and all."

That was the speech, every night, of the Honorable Fred S. Walcott, Esquire, who was duly decked out in a high hat, wing-type collar with a wide bow tie, Prince Albert coat, striped pants and spats, no matter how hot the weather. That ended the parade, and we'd go walk back to the Pullman.

Every night, about 15 minutes before the show would begin, the band gave a little concert in front of the tent. We played popular songs then, but everything was so fast. We'd play about four or five songs and then the audience would be invited to go into the tent to see the show.

The show cost about 75 cents to get in, and you could get a reserved seat for a quarter more. For the opening act of the show, we played what would be called the overture, consisting of a medley of a few popular pieces arranged by Mark Veal, who acted as the orchestra director during the show. After the overture, the grand opening was next. The orchestra would go into a fast number, and the curtain would be drawn back, revealing the entire troupe. At either end of the stage would be comedians in black face, which we called the end men. Next would be the side men and women. There would be two or three couples on both sides of the stage. The chorus girls wore little short dresses and lots of makeup. The interlocutor would be seated in an elevated chair just a little above the other members of the troupe. After a spirited song by the entire cast, the interlocutor would step forward and greet the audience. He would more or less outline the type of performance to be presented. At this juncture, the star or stars as the case may be would come to the center of the stage and either sing or engage the interlocutor in a conversation of a comic nature. Charlie Rue was the interlocutor, and Rich Brown was the first star that came out, and he would get hearty laughs out of the audience when he described his experience in taking a bath.

Charlie would say, "How you feel, Rich?"

Rich would say, "Oh, I feel bad. I feel terrible."

"What seems to be your trouble?"

"Lord, Charlie, I took a bath. That thing nearly killed me."

"What you mean it nearly killed you?"

"I never felt so cold in all my life. That water nearly killed me. I swear to God, I'll never get in another wash pan of water as long as I live."

That kind of encounter would always get big laughs. The opening would be concluded with another song with the entire cast taking a part. There would be another round of applause when the curtain was drawn. Other acts would then follow, such as acrobats, specialties, and skits. All during the show, the orchestra would play the songs that were sung by the performers, and the ones the dancers danced to, and during the other acts. The band would have music going the whole time, and the show would last between 1½ – 2 hours. The band was not on the stage, but we were seated immediately in front of what is normally called the pit area in the theater.

Two of our specialty acts were Barrel and the Great Adams. Barrel's act was to jump into a fiery barrel, fully clothed, then jump out of the barrel wearing only his shorts. The Great Adams would wear a little tiny straw hat. He'd be in black face with a dead pan sad expression that never changed. He would come out on stage riding a bicycle. He would perform several acts with the bicycle, raring up and riding on the rear wheel. Then he would detach the handlebars and keep riding. Next he would detach the front wheel and ride on the rear wheel. He would then detach the frame and ride it as a unicycle. He would dance to the music while on the unicycle.

The grand finale was like the opening act with everyone out on stage. After some songs, there would be dancing and someone like Sweet Georgia Brown with a beautiful voice would sing a final song, something like "Swanee River," and the curtain would drop. As a rule, following the regular performance, there was extra entertainment at an after-show, or concert. Remaining in the tent for the concert cost about 50 cents. It was the same kind of act, just more of it, for about 30 minutes. Sometimes a dance would be held at a hall in the town. The orchestra would play for these dances and it would cost another 50 cents admission.

We had advancemen for the show. Somebody would go along about two weeks or a month before the show came through to arrange for a lot on which to put the show. Some of the towns levied taxes, which had to be paid before the show could come into town. Then there were two or three men who came through later to place signs on billboards and houses to announce the arrival of the minstrel show. The canvas boys erected the show. They were two or three able-bodied men who could erect the tent, place the seats in it, and erect the stage, and they could do this within four hours after the show hit town. The tent was large enough to seat at least 300 people. All those seats could be moved and placed back in the railroad car along with the tent and other equipment within three hours after the show closed.

Some white people came to the shows. Usually, about one-third of the audience was white—segregated, of course. Whites were always on the right side. We used to say "goats to the left, and the sheep over there."

One of the older performers told me that I would like Durham. He said the parade would go right down the main colored street, Fayetteville Street, and end up at the Elks Club. He said, "Now you're going to see something this time. Everyone is going to be glad to see us." We got out there all decked out in our uniforms and were so happy marching down the street to the Elks Club. North Carolina Central College was in Durham, and it was also the home of North Carolina Mutual Insurance Company. There were a lot of very intelligent black people in Durham, and it turned out that they frowned upon minstrel shows and anything that had to do with minstrel shows. We marched up to the Elks Club and there were several men sitting on the porch. We formed a circle and tore into "Princess of India Overture." As we finished, we expected a loud applause. Nothing happened. The men continued talking among themselves. No applause. No one even looked in our direction. I said to myself, "What the heck is going on here?" It seems that the more intelligent blacks were looking upon the minstrel show as a throwback to slavery and everything relating to slavery. I became more disenchanted at that very moment, as I was having a lot of trouble getting in on the music and a hard time even living from day to day. I hadn't had a bath since I left home.

We played the little town of Albemarle, North Carolina, where all of the white folks lived on one side of the railroad tracks and the blacks lived on the other. Barrel and I looked all over the colored section and finally came to a rundown two-story house where the proprietor said we could sleep that night.

We did our performance in Albemarle and after the show we found our way back across the tracks and up the hill to the lodging house. When we got there we found a great commotion going on. It seemed that a guy by the name of Boll Weevil had caught some boy running around with his girlfriend and had promised to go home and get his shotgun, bring it back and blow the hell out of the damn place. Now, I had never been exposed to anything like that, but everybody was laughing about it.

"It's going to be something," somebody said. "You just wait around here. When old Boll Weevil gets back, he is going to raise some hell."

I said, "Barrel, let's go to bed. Let's get out of here right quick."

So we went on to bed. I didn't sleep that night, though Boll Weevil never did come back to raise all that hell. I was curled up in a knot waiting for him to get back until broad daylight. We had to get up at 6 a.m. in order to catch the train, which was leaving at 6:30. I got going so fast that I didn't have a chance to wash up, but I found out that most of the guys on the car didn't do much bathing, either. I started to understand why minstrel performers traveling from town to town were looked upon with such disfavor. We caught the train just as it was pulling out. It was about a two and a half hour ride to the next town where we were to do another show. I soon found myself asleep standing up.

When I got to the next town I got off the train and found myself a nice shady tree and took a short nap. Buck woke me up to eat breakfast and the same thing repeated that day in finding a room. We were showing in High Point, North Carolina that night and before the parade I found the telegraph office and wired Mama to send me $50 so that I could go back home.

I told Buck, "I'm leaving this mess. I'm going home."

He said, "Well, Quig, don't leave right now. When you get your money, just keep it and stick around until the man fires you. Then leave. I wouldn't leave or walk off. I wouldn't quit. I'd make him fire me. If you quit, he might make you pay him back for the ticket to Greensboro."

That sounded pretty good to me. Anyway, we were getting farther and farther from Mississippi all the time. I went back to the telegraph office about 4:00 p.m. and my $50 was there. I took the money and put it inside my sock and kept that sock on until we got to Danville, Virginia, where Mr. Walcott asked Buck to inform me that I was fired.

I was so glad to be fired I didn't know what to do. I did not report for the parade. I went straight to the railroad station and waited for that Southern Railroad train to take me back to Meridian, Mississippi, where I could take an Illinois Central to Vicksburg, and the Y. & M.V. from Vicksburg to Port Gibson. I got back there a very despondent young man, though I was glad to be home.

True enough, Port Gibson was a small town and the main industry was farming. There was a sawmill and a cottonseed oil mill that always smelled just like peanuts. And there was a big compress where cotton was pressed into small bales. Other than that, everything else was farming. There were some stores, a lot of churches, white people and black people. Although

Milton Quigless in 1980.

segregation was strictly enforced and there was Jim Crow on every hand, and you couldn't vote and had to listen to speeches by the white men running for office saying their main pitch was to keep the nigger in his place, it was much better than the situations I had encountered as a musician in the minstrel band, and I was glad to be back there.

The first thing I did was take a bath. I was in the tub one solid hour before I felt clean. The next thing was eating. I thought I would never fill up on that home cooked meal, so I had two. When I got to bed, I slept fourteen hours. Since I was so despondent, my parents gave me a lot of consolation and helped build up my self-confidence again. When I got back to Alcorn, I told the fellows that the job didn't work out and I just had to quit. When Buck came back to school, however, he explained the situation to my schoolmates. He told them that since he had been on the show before, he had a berth, didn't have to run all the way across town to catch the train, didn't have to stand in the aisle from town to town, and didn't have to contend with abuse from the townspeople wherever we stopped. Therefore, he had been able to survive better than I had. That helped a little, and in about two months, I was my old self again.

Belhaven City Hall and museum.

SINGING THE SMITHSONIAN INSTITUTE BLUES IN BELHAVEN, N.C. EVA BLOUNT WAY'S OWN BELIEVE-IT-OR-NOT MUSEUM

TOM PATTERSON

ONE of the more memorable experiences of my childhood was a visit to the late Robert Ripley's "Believe-It-or-Not" Museum in St. Augustine, Florida, during a family vacation circa 1960. The museum was located in an extravagant stone Victorian mansion with castle-like turrets and ornate iron- and woodwork, and its contents included genuine shrunken human heads from the Amazon, torture instruments from the Spanish Inquisition, a stuffed two-headed calf, meticulously constructed matchstick ships-in-bottles, a replica of Abraham Lincoln's birthplace made of pennies, and hundreds of other strange and exotic items. I was highly intrigued by all this—so much so that if I had had my way, I would have spent every waking hour of that vacation trip roaming the halls of the Ripley collection instead of frolicking on the beach.

View of museum from balcony.

I had occasion to recall that fond memory last spring when I traveled across North Carolina to the sleepy little fishing village of Belhaven, located in Beaufort County, N.C., a few miles inland from Pamlico Sound on the Pungo River and the Intracoastal Waterway. I had come to this town of 2,400 citizens to see its undisputed main attraction, a singular institution prosaically known as the Belhaven Memorial Museum. A kind of funky, low-rent version of the famous Ripley collection, it is without question one of the most unusual museums in the United States. Accompanying me on this expedition was the globe-trotting photographer Roger Manley, whose mission was to document the experience on film while I gathered material for an essay that would attempt to explain this idiosyncratic small-town Smithsonian to the outside world.

The Belhaven Memorial Museum is located in the old bell-tower-topped firehouse building on East Main Street, right in the heart of town. Above the three arched doorways in its red brick facade, from left to right, are the painted legends "MUSEUM," "CITY HALL" and "BELHAVEN POLICE DEPT." The police department and other town government offices share the building's ground floor, while the museum occupies the entire loft-like second story. Below the "MUSEUM" sign outside is a pair of heavy wooden doors painted bright blue. Opening these, the visitor follows a stairway leading up to the right and, arriving at the top, enters a maze-like, hodge-podge display of thousands of artifacts, odds-and-ends and outlandish items covering 7,700 square feet of floor space.

Among the objects to be marveled at here are a pair of fleas dressed in microscopic bride-and-groom garb, a huge barnacle-studded ship's anchor from the early 1800s, a dress made for a 700-pound woman, an iron swastika stolen from a German farmhouse during the days of the Third Reich, more than 30,000 buttons, pickled human fetuses and grotesquely deformed animal embryos in jars, an ingrown toenail, a Brazil-nut pod, a pair of petrified walrus tusks alleged to be over 100 million years old, a necktie made from a rattlesnake hide, a 10-pound fibroid tumor removed from a woman at Pungo District Hospital, dozens of old Mason jars full of canned fruit, a piece of wood from the battleship "Constitution," a soccer-ball-size ball of twine from the tops of old feed bags, an iron wash-pot full of dried gourds, a drill with which a local man was electrocuted

Cyclops pigs and two-headed pig.

Dressed fleas, mummified squirrel,
snake that swallowed a wooden egg and died.

while standing in a puddle of water, a bowl full of canceled checks made out to the Red Cross and other charities during the 1940s and '50s, stacks of cans and boxes containing old household products, several piles of old car license plates, the front page of an 1865 newspaper carrying a headline about Abraham Lincoln's assassination, a wreath of imitation flowers made of human hair, a map of Vietnam made out of brightly colored drinking straws, a basket made from an armadillo shell, a porcelain bedpan, a stone reportedly taken from the crumbled walls of Jericho, the skin of an unborn calf, the rib of a whale, a 1909 Edison gramophone, a 1918 German machine gun, a stuffed peacock from the farm of a former Belhaven mayor, a watch fob made from a piece of the first transatlantic cable, hundreds of colorful metal tags from old plug tobacco pouches, a fragment of a spacecraft found off the Bahamas, a boot cut from the leg of a dead Prussian guard during World War I, a set of bookends made of stones removed from the White House during its 1950 renovation, the ornate patchwork jacket of a Seminole Indian chief, a mummified squirrel, rows of old typewriters and high-button shoes, huge posters of silver-screen stars Rudolph Valentino and Jean Harlow, a pair of Howdy Doody glasses, and a spitoon disguised as a turtle.

The building was constructed in 1910, and the second floor was originally used as a theater where silent movies were shown and traveling minstrel acts appeared. Later it was converted into a high-school gym, and the painted basketball-court markers are still visible on the creaking hardwood floor. Suspended from the 25-foot pressed-metal ceiling are eight wood-paddle fans (the museum's warm-weather climate control system) and about a dozen fluorescent light fixtures held up by cords and chains.

Watching over the museum on the afternoon that Roger Manley and I dropped in was Bettie Holloway, a 67-year-old Beaufort County native recently returned to Belhaven after spending most of her life as a medical technician in Houston, Texas. A knowledgeable and sophisticated lady, she displayed a wry sense of humor as she led us on an impromptu tour, pointing out items of particular interest, answering our questions, recounting stories associated with some of the objects in the collection, and providing an interesting account of the life of the woman responsible for assembling all this stuff under one roof.

One of the rattlers Mrs. Way killed.

Eva Blount was born in 1869, the day after Christmas, in Pantego, a nearby Beaufort County community. Her family, the Blounts, was one of the most prominent in Eastern North Carolina, with a distinguished ancestry that can be traced back 12 centuries prior to her birth—a family tree that includes Danish and English royalty, American shipping magnates and Revolutionary War heroes. At 17 she married a local lumber company owner named Harvey Rowland Way and moved to the 145-acre farm where she lived for the rest of her life, about five miles outside Belhaven.

Eva Blount Way—or "Mrs. Eva," as she was known locally—was remarkable not so much because of her lineage as because of what she did with her life. While her late husband once described her as "a child who found it virtually impossible to grow up," a 1951 entry in the Washington (N.C., not D.C.) *Daily News* summed her up as "housewife, snakekiller, curator, trapper, dramatic actress, philosopher and preserver of all the riches of mankind," as well as "the most fascinating person you can imagine." The latter accolade might be something of an overstatement, but it's at least safe to say that she was *one* of the most fascinating characters of her time and place—Eastern North Carolina in the waning years of the 19th and the first half of the 20th centuries.

Mrs. Way started Beaufort County's first country club and was president of the local DAR chapter. She won more blue ribbons for canning home-grown fruits and vegetables than any other woman in the county. She was a poet. She beat ten men in a hog-calling contest at the county fair. She hunted rattlesnakes with a garden hoe and made a point of killing four or five of them a year, always saving their skins and rattles. She trapped and killed a bear that had been eating her corn crop, then she canned and ate him, piece by piece, until all that was left was a claw that is still enshrined in her collection. And that, of course, was the most remarkable thing about this "fascinating person"—her constantly growing collection of the bizarre and the commonplace.

In a 1956 interview she remembered that when she married and moved into her farmhouse, "there were no pictures on the walls, no objects on the mantels," so "I decided to start collecting something to make the place more interesting. Then I became interested in curious objects. I have never thrown anything away."

Rembrandt and governess.

In 1940 she opened her home to the public as "Mrs. Way's Museum," making the collection accessible to anyone who cared to visit it for his or her own entertainment and edification. There was no admission fee; instead, there was a donation box in which visitors could deposit whatever amount they thought the experience was worth (a practice that continues to this day at the collection's new home). Mrs. Way inaugurated her museum in the wake of the United States' entry into World War II, as a means of raising funds for the Red Cross and other charitable organizations that were mobilized to support the "war effort." She continued to pass on all proceeds to these and other charities up until the time of her death in the early 1960s.

Her reputation spread throughout Beaufort County, Eastern North Carolina and beyond, and people she had never heard of began bringing and sending her objects they thought were interesting or unusual enough to be enshrined in her museum, which, along with its more exotic contents, also included such mundane commercial specimens as a box of Boraxine soap powder, a cake of Octagon soap, two bottles of Black Silk stove polish, a tin of Clabber Girl baking powder, seven boxes of Champion Cup shaving soap, a container of Movie Girl beauty powder and a box of Mulliken's Vermifuge for expelling the large round worm in children.

Pointing out one of the old woodstoves now housed in the Belhaven Memorial Museum, Bettie Holloway noted, "Mrs. Way had five stoves in her kitchen at the time of her death. I don't know how many of them were operating, but that just goes to show you that she was telling the truth when she said she never threw anything away."

There are varying accounts of how some of these curiosities made their way into the collection. For example, Holloway said one rumor has it that the fleas in wedding attire—one of the museum's most popular displays—were dressed by Mrs. Way in collaboration with "some Indian that she knew." Another story, however, has it that these formally-clothed insects were given to Mrs. Way by a band of gypsies passing through Beaufort County many years ago.

"Mrs. Eva" lived to the ripe old age of 93, and her collection continued to grow with each passing year. Soon after her death in 1962, it literally

Re-assembled skeleton.

took on a life of its own. Her will left her estate to her daughter, Catherine Way Wilkinson, who sold off a variety of pieces from the collection during the two to three years it was in her hands. In 1964 Wilkinson was offered $3,000 for the remaining items by a man who owned a museum on nearby Ocracoke Island, and she was about to make the transaction when his offer was bettered by a group of Belhaven citizens who wanted to keep Mrs. Way's strange legacy in their community. Thus was born the Belhaven Memorial Museum. The collection was removed from the Way farmhouse and installed in a Belhaven storefront, where it opened its doors on April Fool's Day, 1965. Two years later, when the old firehouse was renovated and its ground floor converted into town offices, the museum was relocated to its present home upstairs, where it continues to grow as new artifacts and curiosities are donated. The Belhaven town government provides the space rent-free and picks up the utility bills. The museum itself is an independent, non-profit corporation administered by a local board of directors and staffed in part with funds from the Mid-East Commission, a federal grant program designed to provide employment opportunities for senior citizens like Bettie Holloway. Visitors can tour the collection seven days a week from 1 to 5 p.m.

Part of the Belhaven Memorial Museum's appeal is its down-home, non-professional ambience. Items in the collection are labeled with stained and yellowed index cards and paper scraps containing information written out by hand or typed on an ancient typewriter and attached to objects, walls and shelves with Scotch tape, carpet tacks or straight pins. Everything is organized without apparent rhyme or reason and crowded into old drugstore display cabinets, piled up on tabletops, crammed into bookshelves, strewn on the floors, and hung from the walls and ceiling. The random juxtapositions of objects often border on the surreal. Look to your right and there are shelves lined with jars of pickled tumors, fetuses, and snakes; and here on the left we have more than 100 different kinds of foreign currency. Here's a Chinese opium pipe displayed alongside a large quartz crystal donated by Oral Roberts and a rusty metal lancet attached to an index card bearing the handwritten explanation, "Used to bleed people." On a high shelf above these curios, at the feet of a headless department-store dummy wearing a Victorian dress that once belonged

Rattles and accessories from snakes killed by Mrs. Way.

to the wife of the president of the first Peruvian railroad, is a big glass jar stuffed with tickets to the 1930 Coastal Plain Fair in Tarboro, North Carolina. Touring this place is a bit like wandering through a theater-size Joseph Cornell assemblage box or a vast Edward Kienholz installation.

There has been some talk among the museum's directors and other local community leaders of reorganizing the displays, imposing some sensible order on all the marvelously chaotic clutter and otherwise "professionalizing" the place. A "comprehensive study" of the museum prepared in 1980 by a consultant made a number of recommendations along those lines: "The random method of display must be corrected for educational purposes," the report asserts, then goes on to suggest "the classification of items into appropriate categories" and "a system of labeling that will be legible and consistent."

While no doubt well-intentioned and professionally sound, such recommendations overlook the obvious fact that this museum is of interest as much because of its crazy-quilt form as its anything-goes content. It draws four- to five-thousand curiosity-seekers a year precisely because it *isn't* your average, standardized, sophisticated, carefully organized, well-lit, bureaucratically administered regional heritage museum. Visiting this uniquely funky institution is more like exploring some huge and musty old attic than touring the local history museum—and much more entertaining and surprise-filled. Fortunately all suggestions for reorganizing and relabeling the collection have thus far gone unheeded.

"The newest thing we've gotten is that great big whale skull over there," Bettie Holloway explains, pointing to the impressive artifact. "That was donated just this past November by William Tate. He's a local fisherman here, and he caught that skull in his net one day when he was out trawling." Then she adds, with the clear implication that not all curiosities are as welcome as this whale skull, "We've had to start discouraging some donations lately, because as you can see, we don't really have much more room left up here."

The Belhaven Memorial Museum is a latter-day American *kunst-und-wunder-kammer*. Say what? That's right: *kunst-und-wunder-kammer*, which is German for "art-and-wonder-room," a tradition started in the 18th century when many of Europe's wealthier citizens began visiting the far

Marine exhibit (whale skull and anchor).

reaches of their nations' colonial empires and returning home with various curios and other souvenir items they had gathered in the course of their travels. They would set aside special rooms in their houses for displaying these things, and the earliest museums evolved as public versions of these interestingly cluttered rooms. Although she was a stay-at-home type who didn't travel to exotic lands, Eva Blount Way established an ever-expanding network of people who did, whether for their own pleasure or under U.S. military auspices, and the objects they picked up in these distant locations often wound up in her collection, where they can still be seen to this day.

The trip to the Belhaven Museum last spring was my second. My introduction to the place was four years earlier, and I was accompanied by Roger Manley on that excursion as well. It was a memorable trip for several reasons in addition to the museum.

Roger and I had just spent a couple of days on Hatteras Island, on North Carolina's Outer Banks, with the late Annie Hooper, listening to this diminutive white-haired lady's oddly childlike voice as she guided us through her house filled with 5,000 pieces of biblically-inspired driftwood sculpture that she had been working on for 40 years. That in itself was an experience to rival the Belhaven Museum. The next morning, after a rough crossing to the mainland on the storm-tossed Pamlico Sound Ferry—a 25-mile ordeal which took several hours and which Roger aptly compared to "something right out of *Captain's Courageous*"—we drove into Belhaven in Roger's van looking for the museum.

As we pulled up at a stop sign and looked around for someone who might give us directions, who should appear directly in front of us but a peculiar-looking man riding a bicycle across the handlebars of which was balanced a primitive handmade model of a U.S. Navy battleship. We managed to get his attention, and he stopped his bike on the sidewalk as we parked the van and got out. We introduced ourselves—his name was Jimmy Courson—and momentarily forgot all about asking directions while we admired the roughly-crafted, handpainted model ship, which he proudly explained that he had made after seeing the full-size version at a nearby naval base. It was a classic piece of American folk art, no question about it. As for Jimmy, he was even more curious-looking at close range

Button collection.

than when we had first spotted him. Dressed rather like a postman in a summer uniform—pale blue short-sleeved shirt, dark short pants, black socks and shiny leather shoes—he had dark, slicked-back hair, childlike eyes and one of the most impressive sets of buck teeth I've ever seen. He looked like he was maybe in his mid-thirties, but he talked more like a somewhat shy 10-year-old. He told us that if we liked this ship, we might like to see the other ones he had at home. That sounded good to us, so we got back in the van and followed along as he slowly pedaled through a quiet, oak-shaded neighborhood to a small suburban-ranch-style brick house with a rickety old wood-frame garage out back.

Jimmy lived with his elderly parents, who maintained a ghostly reticence during our brief meeting with them before we headed out to the garage which Jimmy used as his workshop and display area. Sure enough, he had about a dozen more handmade models in there—mostly ships of various kinds, but there was also a helicopter on a miniature ocean-based landing platform—and every one of them had the same compelling raw-and-rough-hewn look that we had admired in the battleship he had been carrying around on his bicycle. Roger and I spent about an hour inspecting these and taking photographs of Jimmy with his creations. He seemed to appreciate the attention, and he even took off his shoes and waded into the narrow canal behind his house with one of the ships, which he set down on the water's surface to demonstrate its seaworthiness. Finally, not wanting to overstay our welcome, we told him we had to be getting along. And, by the way, we asked him if he could tell us how to find the Belhaven Memorial Museum. He said he didn't know, that he had never been to a museum, but that he thought he might have heard something about a museum somewhere in town. He was clearly a man who lived in his own little world.

We managed to find the museum a few minutes later, only a block from where we had first seen Jimmy Courson on his bicycle. After stopping for lunch in a little cafe around the corner, we walked up the street, through the blue doors under the "MUSEUM" sign, up the creaky stairs of the old Belhaven firehouse building and into the fabulously incongruous and profusely cluttered world of Eva Blount Way.

Late that afternoon as we drove westward out of town on U.S. 264,

Roger and I were both still shaking our heads in amazement at the unexpected marvels to be encountered in these seemingly normal little towns along the Southern backroads.

I was having similar thoughts after this most recent visit to Belhaven as we hit the road back to more urban environs. And I was thinking back on that childhood trip to the Ripley's Museum in St. Augustine. And, for some reason, a couple of lines from an old song by Don Van Vliet (a.k.a. Captain Beefheart) were running through my head again and again like a repeating tape loop:

> *The new dinosaur's walkin' in the old one's shoes,*
> *singin' the Smithsonian Institute Blues!*

CONTRIBUTOR'S NOTES

ALEX ALBRIGHT grew up in Graham and received degrees from UNC-Chapel Hill and UNC-Greensboro. He has edited three volumes of poetry: *The North Carolina Poems* by A. R. Ammons, *Dreaming the Blues: Poems from Martin County Prison*, and *Leaves of Greens: The Collard Poems*. He is an Assistant Professor of English at East Carolina University, where he is editor of the *North Carolina Literary Review*.

STANLEY KNICK received his B.A. from UNC-Greensboro, and his M.A. and Ph.D. from Indiana University. He is the Director of Native American Resource Center and Research Assistant Professor in American Indian Studies at Pembroke State University. His research interests include Native American prehistory, culture, and health.

ROGER MANLEY, photographer, folklorist, and gardener, is curator for the Meta Museum and the American Visionary Art Museum in Baltimore. He has collaborated in book projects with Reynolds Price *(Home Made)* and Shelby Stephenson *(Plankhouse)*.

TOM PATTERSON is the author of *St. EOM in The Land of Pasaquan* (Jargon, 1987) and *Howard Finster, Stranger from Another World* (Abbeville Press, 1989), editor of *Art Vu*, and visual arts columnist for the Winston-Salem *Journal*.

DR. MILTON D. QUIGLESS, SR. is a graduate of Meharry Medical College. He is Director of the Quigless Clinic in Tarboro, North Carolina, where he has practiced medicine since the mid-1930s. This excerpt is from his unpublished autobiography, *Looking Back*.

J. CHRIS WILSON is Professor of Art at Barton College. A studio artist, represented in many public and private collections, he teaches studio art and art history, including American material culture, and has lectured extensively on architecture and the decorative arts in Eastern North Carolina.